Praise for *Inside the Minds*

"This series provides a practical and focused discussion of the leading issues in law today." – John V. Biernacki, Partner, Jones Day

"*Inside the Minds* draws from the collective experience of the best professionals. The books are informative from an academic, and, more importantly, practical perspective. I highly recommend them." – Keith M. Aurzada, Partner, Bryan Cave LLP

"Aspatore's *Inside the Minds* series provides practical, cutting edge advice from those with insight into the real world challenges that confront businesses in the global economy." – Michael Bednarek, Partner, Shearman & Sterling LLP

"What to read when you want to be in the know—topical, current, practical, and useful information on areas of the law that everyone is talking about." – Erika L. Morabito, Partner, Patton Boggs LLP

"Some of the best insight around from sources in the know" – Donald R. Kirk, Shareholder, Fowler White Boggs PA

"The *Inside the Minds* series provides a unique window into the strategic thinking of key players in business and law." – John M. Sylvester, Partner, K&L Gates LLP

"Comprehensive analysis and strategies you won't find anywhere else." – Stephen C. Stapleton, Of Counsel, Dykema Gossett PLLC

"The *Inside the Minds* series is a real hands-on, practical resource for cutting edge issues." – Trey Monsour, Partner, Haynes and Boone LLP

"A tremendous resource, amalgamating commentary from leading professionals that is presented in a concise, easy to read format." – Alan H. Aronson, Shareholder, Akerman Senterfitt

"Unique and invaluable opportunity to gain insight into the minds of experienced professionals." – Jura C. Zibas, Partner, Lewis Brisbois Bisgaard & Smith LLP

"A refreshing collection of strategic insights, not dreary commonplaces, from some of the best of the profession." – Roger J. Magnuson, Partner, Dorsey & Whitney LLP

"Provides valuable insights by experienced practitioners into practical and theoretical developments in today's ever-changing legal world." – Elizabeth Gray, Partner, Willkie, Farr & Gallagher LLP

"This series provides invaluable insight into the practical experiences of lawyers in the trenches." – Thomas H. Christopher, Partner, Kilpatrick Stockton LLP

ASPATORE

www.Aspatore.com

Aspatore Books, a Thomson Reuters business, exclusively publishes C-Level executives (CEO, CFO, CTO, CMO, Partner) from the world's most respected companies and law firms. C-Level Business Intelligence™, as conceptualized and developed by Aspatore Books, provides professionals of all levels with proven business intelligence from industry insiders—direct and unfiltered insight from those who know it best—as opposed to third-party accounts offered by unknown authors and analysts. Aspatore Books is committed to publishing an innovative line of business and legal books, those which lay forth principles and offer insights that when employed, can have a direct financial impact on the reader's business objectives. In essence, Aspatore publishes critical tools for all business professionals.

Inside the Minds

The *Inside the Minds* series provides readers of all levels with proven legal and business intelligence from C-Level executives and lawyers (CEO, CFO, CTO, CMO, Partner) from the world's most respected companies and law firms. Each chapter is comparable to a white paper or essay and is a future-oriented look at where an industry, profession, or topic is heading and the most important issues for future success. Each author has been selected based upon their experience and C-Level standing within the professional community. *Inside the Minds* was conceived in order to give readers actual insights into the leading minds of top lawyers and business executives worldwide, presenting an unprecedented look at various industries and professions.

INSIDE THE MINDS

Mortgage and Finance Fraud Litigation Strategies

Leading Lawyers on Managing the Complexities of Fraud Cases, Understanding Government Regulations, and Structuring an Effective Litigation Plan

ASPATORE

Mat #41072776

Inside the Minds Project Manager, Tiffany Smith; edited by Jo Alice Darden; proofread by Melanie Zimmerman

ISBN 978-0-314-26825-9

For corrections, updates, comments or any other inquiries please e-mail TLR.AspatoreEditorial@thomson.com.

First Printing, 2010
10 9 8 7 6 5 4 3 2 1

CONTENTS

Strategies for Effective Mortgage Insurance Litigation

David E. Weiss

Partner

Reed Smith LLP

ASPATORE

Introduction

The focus of my practice is representing corporate policyholders in disputes with their insurance companies. I also advise clients on insurance issues that arise in the course of various corporate transactions, as well as issues pertaining to insurance policy renewals.

I have engaged in this practice almost exclusively for the past twenty years. My practice includes representing financial institutions, such as securities broker dealers and banks, in connection with insurance disputes. Over the past year-and-a-half, I have been representing various lending institutions in connection with disputes over coverage under mortgage insurance policies sold to protect against loan defaults. These disputes have resulted in numerous lawsuits and arbitration proceedings and involve coverage for individual mortgage loans, as well as pools of mortgage loans that were placed into various mortgage-backed securities, including subprime mortgages.

These controversies have come about because of the financial crisis, including the steep decline in home values. The huge increase in mortgage loan defaults has resulted in a huge increase in mortgage insurance claims. Faced with the prospect of having to pay out vast sums in response to these claims, mortgage insurers began to deny claims at an unprecedented rate, in some cases seeking to rescind mortgage insurance altogether based on allegations of fraud. This has led to the current litigation between mortgage insurers and lenders.

In addition to handling litigation matters, I and other members of our insurance recovery group at Reed Smith have developed an in-depth understanding regarding the workings of the mortgage market, including the mortgage origination process, securitizations, alleged mortgage fraud, and the process for submitting and handling mortgage insurance claims. By understanding the business aspects, we are better able to effectively handle and resolve litigation matters for our clients. For example, I can say that I have read from cover to cover (more than once) the *Uniform Standards of Appraisal Practice,* which has allowed me to better understand the appraisal process so that I can effectively and efficiently deal with issues concerning alleged appraisal misrepresentation, which have become a large focus of disputes between lenders and their mortgage insurers. I also have reviewed hundreds of individual loan files to better understand the myriad of issues that arise in the context of a mortgage insurance dispute. Without this detailed knowledge base, it would be more difficult to represent clients in an effective and efficient manner.

Mortgage Insurance and Cases: An Overview

Mortgage insurance is designed to protect lenders and other owners of mortgage loans against the risk of borrower defaults. A typical definition of mortgage insurance is found at CAL. INS. CODE § 119 (2005), which provides that mortgage insurance "includes insurance against financial loss by reason of the nonpayment of principal, interest and other sums agreed to be paid under the terms of any note or bond or other evidence of indebtedness secured by a mortgage, deed of trust, or other instrument constituting a lien or charge on real estate."

In most cases, mortgage insurance covers a percentage of the loss, typically as high as 40 percent. Mortgage insurance can be paid by borrowers as part of their monthly payment, or it can be paid directly by the lender with the cost passed along to the borrower, typically in the form of a higher interest payment. Mortgage insurance is needed where the borrower puts down less than 20 percent. For instance, both Fannie Mae and Freddie Mac generally cannot acquire new mortgages with less than 20 percent down unless there is mortgage insurance. As one mortgage insurer explains, "[m]ajor investors that supply liquidity to the mortgage market, such as Fannie Mae and Freddie Mac, require credit enhancements [mortgage insurance] on loans with loan-to-value ratios over 80 percent in order to diversify risk and help ensure the stability of the mortgage finance system." PMI Group Inc., *Company Profile* (Sept. 2009), available at www.pmi-us.com/media/pdf/nes/Company Profile.pdf.

Thus, for loans with less than 20 percent down, mortgage insurance is needed for lenders to be able to sell loans to the secondary market. If lenders could not sell loans to secondary market investors, the capacity to originate new loans would be diminished. As one mortgage insurer, United Guaranty, explained on its Web site in 2006: "The mortgage guaranty insurance provided by United Guaranty Residential Insurance Company ...

does more than protect the lenders who finance homes. It allows home buyers throughout the country to fulfill dreams that would be impossible to achieve without mortgage insurance." In a 2005 press release announcing an initiative to provide mortgage insurance products and services in Mexico to help increase home ownership opportunities for Mexico's citizens, United Guaranty further explained:

> Mortgage guaranty products provide loss protection to lenders and investors in case of borrower default on residential mortgage loans. Home ownership studies show that loans with limited down payments have an increased likelihood of default, particularly in periods of severe or prolonged economic distress. As housing finance systems develop around the world, credit risk for low down payment mortgages is a major challenge in expanding home ownership.

In addition to facilitating the sale of mortgages to the secondary market, including Fannie and Freddie, mortgage insurance has been used to facilitate the securitization of mortgage loans by providing "credit enhancement" for residential mortgage-backed securities.

What Is to Blame for Increased Mortgage Loan Defaults and Resulting Insurance Claims?

Mortgage insurers argue that they do not insure against mortgage loan defaults where there was fraud in the loan origination. Thus, the mortgage insurers allege that a large percentage of loans under review involved fraud by either the borrowers, by someone involved in the loan origination, or by multiple parties. The mortgage insurers allege that there was systemic fraud, and that this, coupled with improper loosening of underwriting standards, led to the massive and unprecedented increase in mortgage defaults and insurance claims.

While nobody can contend that fraud was non-existent, and it is true that lending standards were relaxed over time through various factors, including governmental policies regarding affordable housing, the mortgage insurers completely ignore the impact of the economy on the increase in mortgage defaults and insurance claims. Rather than rampant fraud, as they allege, the increased level of loan defaults is directly related to the devastating economic recession, including unprecedented unemployment, coupled with the severe depreciation of home values.

Moreover, to the extent that relaxed lending guidelines are to blame, the mortgage insurance industry was involved in their development every step of the way. Mortgage insurers certainly knew about the evolution of loan underwriting guidelines and even encouraged more relaxed standards as a way to increase the number of loans that would require mortgage insurance. After all, one significant way for mortgage insurers to increase their own profits is to make sure there are more and more mortgages to insure. As late as April 2007, PMI's president and chief executive officer (CEO), David Katkov, stated:

> [m]ortgage insurance allows lenders to expand their product offerings for high-LTV loans and further develop the market for first-time buyers, low- to moderate- income borrowers and minorities who may not qualify under traditional FICO, LTV and credit guidelines. This is particularly important in a shrinking market, as the majority share of future market growth is forecast to come from these segments. D. Katkov, *Mortgage Insurance 101*, Mortgage Banking (April 2007).

Mortgage insurers thus promoted their product as an important tool toward the goal of greater home ownership in the United States. Since mortgage insurance is required only when a borrower puts down less than 20 percent, by definition, mortgage insurance applies to the riskier loans on the market. Therefore, mortgage insurance was seen as an important aspect of the nation's goal to expand home ownership, by allowing lenders the ability to provide loans to more riskier borrowers and the ability to sell those loans to secondary market participants, such as Fannie Mae and Freddie Mac, so that capital could be freed up to make more loans available. As one scholar explained in 2005 before the real estate market collapse:

> PMI is an important form of risk sharing that makes lenders more willing to provide mortgage loans for home buyers, especially those home buyers with very limited

cash resources. It also makes higher risk home mortgage loans more salable in the secondary mortgage market and thereby contributes considerably to the volume of securitized mortgages, a large and growing sector of the securities market. The net effect of PMI is that it helps substantially in increasing the percentage of occupant home ownership, particularly for families with lower or moderate incomes. Q. Johnstone, *Private Mortgage Insurance*, 39 Wake Forest Law. Rev. 101, 154 (January 6, 2005).

Certainly, the insurers understood that loans where borrowers provided limited or no documentation to support their incomes and assets, and subprime mortgages provided to lenders with less than stellar credit profiles, would involve a greater risk of default than more traditional loans. Indeed, a review of the trade literature reveals a great deal of discussion regarding the risks associated with these types of loans, including statements from mortgage insurance executives. As early as 2004, for example, United Guaranty reported that stated income loans accounted for 60 percent to 65 percent of its "limited documentation" loans. When United Guaranty compared full documentation and stated income loans with the same credit profiles, stated income loans had delinquency rates that were one to two times higher. Nevertheless, United Guaranty said: "We're OK with that. We take on risk by not getting income verification, but it's a good calculated risk." See Robert Stowe, "Pushing the Edge on Alternative-A," *Mortgage Banking* (Feb. 2004). In another article in March 2004, the president and CEO of Mortgage Guaranty Insurance Corporation (MGIC), said that stated income loans insured by MGIC had five times more risk than full documentation loans. See Curt Culver, "Stating the Obvious about Reduced-doc Risk," *Mortgage Banking* (March 2004).

PMI succinctly described the risks associated with certain loan types in its SEC filings. For instance, in March 2005 PMI stated the following:

> PMI insures less-than-A quality loans and Alt-A loans…. PMI defines less-than-A quality loans to include loans with FICO scores (a credit score provided by Fair, Isaac and Company) generally less than 620. PMI defines Alt-A loans

as loans where the borrower's FICO score is 620 or higher and the loan includes certain characteristics such as reduced documentation verifying the borrower's income, assets, deposit information and/or employment. We expect higher default rates and claim payment rates for high LTV loans, ARMS, less-than-A quality loans and Alt-A loans and incorporate these assumptions into our pricing. PMI Group Inc., Annual Report (Form 10-K), at 10 (March 11, 2005).

So the insurers knew exactly the risks they were undertaking when they agreed to insure these loan products.

Fraud Is Not the Answer

From my perspective, insurance company efforts to prove fraud in most cases fall flat, as the reason for a loan default is more a function of the economic crisis, and the risks inherent in many of the loans for which mortgage insurance was procured. From a practical standpoint, it is difficult for an insurer to prove there was fraud in a particular mortgage, and the evidence often put forth by the mortgage insurers to establish fraud is weak and highly circumstantial.

Where it appears that there might have been fraud, it often involves the borrower and possibly a mortgage broker. Rarely is there evidence of a lender being directly involved in the fraud. While lenders certainly were interested in increasing their business, it is difficult to imagine why lenders would want to encourage borrowers to commit fraud, and lenders spent substantial time and money attempting to root out and eliminate fraud. Further, since mortgage insurers typically insure only a percentage of the loss for a particular loan, there is little incentive for lenders to defraud the insurers. Stories you hear about lenders coaching borrowers about what to put down on a loan application seem overblown. Rather, it appears that borrowers involved with fraud or the brokers they worked with were quite sophisticated in knowing what they needed to do to get their loans approved. In most cases, however, there is no credible evidence of fraud.

Attempts to Rescind Coverage on Pools of Covered Loans by Asserting Fraud in the Inducement

In addition to dealing with claims from mortgage insurers regarding fraud in individual mortgages, we also have been involved with claims by mortgage insurers against lenders alleging fraud in the inducement. Mortgage insurers seek to rescind coverage on a pool-wide basis with regard to insurance placed on pools of loans sold into various securitizations. The insurers claim that the lenders misled the mortgage insurers regarding their loan underwriting practices, and that the lenders purposefully sold their worst originated loans into securitizations.

These claims are not particularly persuasive, as it appears clear that the mortgage insurers had great visibility into lenders' underwriting practices and even encouraged lenders to loosen underwriting standards so that there would be more loans for them to insure. Moreover, the mortgage insurers had the opportunity to individually select the loans they wanted to insure based on detailed information they requested. The insurers also had an opportunity to review any other information regarding the individual loans before agreeing to participate.

United Guaranty Mortgage Indem. Co. v. Countrywide Financial Corp.

In *United Guar. Mortgage Indem. Co. v. Countrywide Fin. Corp.*, 660 F. Supp. 2d 1163 (C.D. Cal. 2006), the court held that such claims for pool wide rescission and fraud in the inducement by a sophisticated mortgage insurance company were "implausible" as a matter of law, and dismissed a mortgage insurer's fraud and rescission claims on a motion to dismiss, after giving the insurer an opportunity to amend its complaint. According to the court, "[n]o reasonable *insurer* would rely upon generalized representations about 'quality' underwriting—especially oral representations." *Id.* at 1189. Further, where insurers are insuring large numbers of loans in a bulk transaction, the court stated that "any reasonable mortgage insurer that (1) was conducting multibillion-dollar bulk transactions and (2) had an express right to audit or sample the underlying loan files before the transactions closed, would engage in some degree of auditing or sampling of the underlying loan files to be insured." *Id.*

Failure to Adhere to Underwriting Guidelines

Mortgage insurers also argue that they have the right to rescind coverage if they determine that a lender failed to adhere to agreed-on underwriting guidelines. A large percentage of mortgage insurance was written pursuant to "delegated underwriting" programs, whereby larger lenders were permitted to determine whether loans met the guidelines agreed to by the insurance company and commit the insurance company to issue insurance. This delegated underwriting model allowed mortgage insurers to insure more and more loans because they did not have to individually underwrite the loans themselves. Of course, the mortgage insurers took the risk that the lenders would not follow appropriate underwriting standards.

Despite giving lenders delegated authority, or as some have said, "lending their pen" to the lenders, the mortgage insurers now argue that they can second-guess the decisions of these lenders by arguing, after a loan has gone into default and a claim has been submitted, that the lender should not have approved the loan to begin with. These arguments, however, conflict with public statements made by the mortgage insurers as to how their delegated underwriting programs were supposed to operate. For instance, in its March 14, 2006, Form 10-K filed with the Securities and Exchange Commission (SEC), Triad Guaranty Inc. stated the following regarding its delegated underwriting program:

> A significant percentage of our new insurance written is underwritten pursuant to a delegated underwriting program. These programs permit certain mortgage lenders to determine whether mortgage loans meet their program guidelines and enable these lenders to commit us to issue mortgage insurance. We may expand the availability of delegated underwriting to additional customers. If an approved lender commits us to insure a mortgage loan, generally, we may not refuse, except in limited circumstances, to insure, or rescind coverage on, that loan even if the lender fails to follow our delegated underwriting guidelines. Even if we terminate a lender's underwriting authority, we remain at risk for any loans

previously insured on our behalf by the lender before that termination. The performance of loans insured through programs of delegated underwriting has not been tested over a period of extended adverse economic conditions, meaning that the program could lead to greater losses than we anticipate. Greater than anticipated losses could have a material adverse effect on our business, financial condition and operating results.

Establishing Material Misrepresentation or Fraud

In my practice area, the standards for establishing fraud or misrepresentation depend on the terms of the particular mortgage insurance contract at issue, as well as state law dealing with rescission of insurance contracts. Because there is no federal regulation of insurance in the United States, laws in each of the fifty states are potentially implicated when dealing with mortgage insurance issues, as the underlying loans involve insurers, lenders, and properties located in many different jurisdictions. For example, in California, issues regarding insurance rescissions for material misrepresentation and fraud are governed by a combination of statutory provisions contained in the California Insurance Code, and case law. For instance, CAL. INS. CODE § 359 provides that if there is a false representation regarding a "material point," the insured party may "rescind the contract from the time the representation becomes false." In addition, if there is concealment of a material fact, the injured party is entitled to rescind whether or not the concealment was intentional. CAL. INS. CODE § 331.

In the insurance context, the materiality of a representation is determined "by the probable and reasonable influence of the facts upon the party to whom the communication is due, informing his estimate of the disadvantages of the proposed contract, or in making his inquiries." CAL. INS. CODE § 334. The test for materiality is whether the information would have caused the underwriter to reject the application, charge a higher premium, or amend the policy terms, had the underwriter known the facts. *Mitchell v. United Nat'l Ins. Co.*, 127 Cal. App. 4th 457, 474 (Cal. Dist. Ct. App. 2005).

Materiality is a subjective test. The critical question is the effect truthful answers should have had on the insurer, not some average reasonable insurer. *See Mitchell*, 127 Cal. App. 4th at 474 (stating, "The materiality of a misrepresentation in an insurance application is determined by its probable and reasonable effect upon the insurer, which is a subjective test, the critical question being the effect truthful answers would have had on the insurer, not on some average reasonable insurer; the misrepresentation need not relate to the loss ultimately claimed by the insured"); see also *Unionamerica Ins. Co. Ltd. v. Fort Miller Group Inc.*, 590 F. Supp. 2d 1254, 1258 (N.D. Cal. 2008) (stating "test of materiality is subjective in sense that critical question is effect truthful answers would have had on particular insurer, not on some average reasonable insurer").

Despite this subjectivity, courts are willing to consider extrinsic facts, such as industry practice, the nature of the information withheld, and the likely practice of the insurance company. For example, the court in *Mitchell v. United National Insurance Company* stated that expert evidence on industry practice could create an issue of fact as to whether a misrepresentation was material. 127 Cal. App. 4th at 477. Moreover, courts have stated that the "trier of fact is not required to believe the 'post mortem' testimony of an insurer's agents that insurance would have been refused had the true facts been disclosed." *Imperial Cas. & Indem. Co. v. Sogomonian*, 198 Cal. App. 3d 169, 181 (Cal. Dist. Ct. App. 1988). Thus, just an insurance company saying something is material does not control the analysis.

Default Contractual Rules

The above-cited California rules, and similar rules in other jurisdictions, can be altered or supplemented by the contracting parties, and most mortgage insurance policies contain express provisions for dealing with allegations of mortgage fraud. As the court explained in *United Guar. Mortgage Indem. Co. v. Countrywide Fin. Corp.*, 660 F. Supp. 2d 1163, 1190-1191 (C.D. Cal. 2009), "these statutes provide default contractual rules" which can be "contracted away, waived, or otherwise impaired." Under some mortgage insurance policies, the insurance company may be entitled to rescind coverage if there was any fraud or misrepresentation in the mortgage transaction, including fraud committed by the borrower, even if the lender had no knowledge of the borrower's fraud. Other policies contain so-called "incontestability" language that provides that the insurance company cannot rescind unless a "first party" had knowledge of or was involved with the borrower's misrepresentation. A "first party" includes the lender, a mortgage broker, an appraiser, and other specified persons in the origination process, other than the borrower or people affiliated with the borrower. For example, Radian Guaranty Inc.'s mortgage insurance policy contains the following "Misrepresentation and Fraud" exclusion:

> Any Loss for which a Claim is made in connection with a Certificate of Insurance issued in reliance upon an Application for Insurance containing any material misstatement, misrepresentation or omission, whether intentional or otherwise or as a result of any act of fraud; provided, however, that unless the Insured had knowledge of or participated in a Third-Party Misrepresentation or Fraud at the time it was made, the Company shall not rescind or deny coverage, or adjust any Claim based on such Third-Party Misrepresentation or Fraud.

In some cases, there is a requirement that the borrower make twelve consecutive mortgage payments, and other times there is "day one" incontestability. The example above from Radian provides "day one" protection. In practice, mortgage insurers have attempted to take advantage of popular sentiment regarding the mortgage industry by seeking to rescind coverage based on scant and largely unpersuasive evidence of fraud or misrepresentation, ignoring the fact that they have the burden of proof to establish all elements of rescission. See *Clarendon Nat'l Ins. Co. v. Ins. Co. of the West*, 442 F. Supp. 2d 914, 921 (E.D. Cal. 2006). "The burden of proof is on the insurer to establish concealment or misrepresentation." 590 F. Supp. 2d 1254, 1259 (N.D. Cal. 2008).

For instance, mortgage insurers often seek to rescind coverage on the basis that the appraisal used to originate the subject loan was faulty, and therefore the value of the property was misrepresented. In these cases, the insurance companies obtain so-called "retrospective" appraisals to look back and value the property as of the origination date. When the retrospective appraiser comes back with a lower value, the insurer will cite that as the "true value" of the property and argue that there was a misrepresentation.

In these cases, the mortgage insurers ignore the well-established principle that a real estate appraisal is an opinion, and that differences of opinion do not constitute fraud or misrepresentation. "Real estate appraisals are generally considered statements of opinion, rather than statements of fact for purposes of fraud or concealment claims...." 26 WILLISTON ON CONTRACTS § 69:8 (4th ed. 2008). "[L]and values cannot be calculated pursuant to a precise formula....The question of land value is generally a matter of opinion only. *Fifty Assocs. v. Prudential Ins. Co.*, 450 F.2d 1007, 1010 (9th Cir. 1971). The Uniform Standards of Professional Appraisal Practice (USPAP) also recognize that appraised value is a matter of opinion, stating that "[v]alue expresses an economic concept. As such it is never a fact but always an opinion of the worth of a property at a given time in accordance with a specific definition of value."

Because there is no such thing as "actual" or "true" value when dealing with a real property appraisal, it seems improper for a mortgage insurer to rescind coverage based merely on retrospective appraisals performed well after origination, which typically raise highly subjective issues regarding the selection of comparable properties and adjustments to comparables, which most often are open to reasonable debate. In many instances, the retrospective appraisals themselves lack credibility or violate professional appraisal standards.

Misrepresentation of Income by Borrower

Another argument typically raised by mortgage insurers is that the borrowers misrepresented their incomes on the loan applications, which gives them the right to rescind coverage. This issue generally arises in the context of "stated income" or other reduced documentation loans that were common in recent years. For a stated income loan, the borrower did not have to provide documentation to support his or her income. Rather, in addition to considering the value of the subject property, the loan originator evaluated other attributes of the borrower besides income, such as employment, credit score and history, assets and liabilities, etc., to determine whether the borrower was an acceptable risk.

Stated income loans were designed for borrowers with hard-to-document income, such as self-employed borrowers or borrowers who earned substantial cash income. Stated income loans were well known to mortgage insurers. The mortgage insurers had their own guidelines for these and other reduced- or limited-documentation loan products, and charged more in premium based on the increased risk. As discussed above, mortgage insurers were well aware of the possibility that borrowers could misrepresent their incomes, but they were willing to take the risk, given the increased premiums they could earn. As United Guaranty said in 2004 when addressing the increased risk of stated income loans: "We're OK with that. We take on risk by not getting income verification, but it's a good, calculated risk." See Robert Stowe, "Pushing the Edge on Alternative-A," *Mortgage Banking* (Feb. 2004).

Now, faced with large numbers of claims, many involving stated income loans, the mortgage insurers will routinely retain investigators in response to a claim, and these investigators will seek to obtain information to try to show that the income on the borrowers' loan applications was inflated, even though the insurers knew of this risk when they agreed to insure the loans and specifically calculated the risk into their pricing. This information comes in many forms, including borrower bankruptcy filings, tax filing information, statements from employers, and borrower interviews. The evidence in many cases does not establish that the borrower's income was misrepresented. Tax filings, for example, reflect a full year of income; whereas, the borrower's loan application is a snapshot in time. So, if the borrower lost his or her job during the year or his or her hours were cut unexpectedly (not unusual events these days), the borrower's tax filing when averaged across an entire year will necessarily come to a lower monthly amount than was represented on the loan application. Tax filings also may not reflect cash income earned by the borrower, or may not reflect a self-employed borrower's true earnings.

A bankruptcy filing is no more persuasive than the loan application, as it is just a statement made by the borrower regarding income, and the borrower has an incentive in a bankruptcy filing to understate earnings. In most cases, the insurance company will provide only the borrower's bankruptcy application and no backup documentation to support the borrower's representations regarding income. Many times, given other information in the loan file, such as the borrower's credit report, it is clear that the borrower could not have made as little as represented on the bankruptcy filing. Often we have proof that the borrower was making thousands of dollars in monthly payments for credit cards, rent, and other items, such that it is completely implausible when the mortgage insurer argues that the borrower was earning only $500 per month, as stated to the bankruptcy court.

Further, in most cases, the only evidence that a "first party" knew the borrower's allegedly true income comes from interviews with the borrowers who invariably state that they provided accurate income information to the lenders, and they do not know why their loan applications included false information, notwithstanding that they signed their loan applications under threat of civil and criminal penalties. These statements are not persuasive, as borrowers who have been caught lying on their loan applications have every incentive to cast blame away from them and onto the loan originator. Yet mortgage insurers have no trouble rescinding coverage based on such non-credible evidence.

Another interesting aspect to the problem is that mortgage insurers are seeking to rescind coverage for stated income loans where they knew in advance that these loans involved more risk and that borrowers might inflate their incomes, and they charged more in premium for the increased risk. They were happy to accept the premium when home prices were appreciating and they did not expect claims, but now that the market has collapsed and claims are rolling in, they wish to avoid their obligations even where there is no link between the alleged misrepresentation and the reason for the loan default. If the insurers wanted to have incomes verified, the time to do that would have been when they agreed to accept premiums and provide insurance—not after a claim is submitted. As one court stated in a recent case involving an insurer attempting to rescind, "the insurer does have a duty to ask the applicant to provide further information if it knows or should know that the application is inaccurate or incomplete." 590 F. Supp. 2d at 1261.

Insurer Willingness to Provide Coverage despite Potential Inaccuracies and Greater Risk

As discussed above, the mortgage insurance industry was fully aware that stated income loan applications might contain inaccurate or incomplete information regarding the borrower's income; yet insurers agreed to provide coverage without asking questions. For instance, in a 2004 article, the president and CEO of Mortgage Guaranty Insurance Corporation (MGIC), one of the largest mortgage insurers, said with regard to stated income and other reduced documentation loans:

> As you can imagine, these loans are riskier and borrowers are charged a premium for them, which begs the question: Why wouldn't a borrower choose to fully document his or her income to ensure he or she is getting the lowest interest rate possible? It may be stating the obvious, but you can't document what you don't have; and in many instances, SI [stated income] and NI [no-income] loan programs are allowing borrowers to do just that. Curt Culver, "Stating the Obvious about Reduced-doc Risk," *Mortgage Banking* (March 1, 2004).

If insurers believed that these loans were riskier, that there were "many instances" of borrower misrepresentation, and yet they agreed to insure them anyway without requiring proof of income, how is it fair for them to seek to deny coverage after a claim is filed when the risk they anticipated comes to fruition? It is because of this that it is only fair to at least require clear proof that the loan originator knew about or participated in the borrower's misrepresentation before the mortgage insurer is allowed to avoid its coverage responsibilities.

Institutions Most Prone to Mortgage Insurance Cases

With regard to my practice area relating to mortgage insurance disputes, it appears that most mortgage lenders large and small have been affected by aggressive positions being taken by mortgage insurers. Many of these disputes have not yet resulted in litigation being filed, although we probably can expect heightened litigation activity in the future.

With regard to brokers, it appears that in some cases mortgage brokers have encouraged or participated in fraud by borrowers. It is difficult to determine how prevalent this was. Borrowers will often say in interviews with investigators that they provided full and complete information to the brokers and that the brokers put false or incomplete information on the loan application. These statements, however, may be difficult to prove or corroborate with any hard evidence.

In the mortgage insurance area, it seems clear that the economic crisis has been the primary cause for the vastly increased number of mortgage defaults and insurance claims. The increased number of claims has caused the insurance companies to be much more aggressive in asserting that borrowers and lenders engaged in fraud as a way to mitigate their exposure to greater than anticipated losses.

Strategies for Mortgage and Finance Fraud Cases

In my practice area (litigation against mortgage insurers on behalf of lenders), we often deal with disputes over thousands of claims in a single lawsuit. Each mortgage loan presents unique facts and circumstances, so the challenge is trying to develop an effective and efficient way to manage the cases without having to litigate each individual loan. Each loan is distinct, but there are common themes at play, so loans can be "bucketed" into different categories. Some raise appraisal issues; others raise issues concerning misrepresentation of income; and others raise still different issues. Hopefully, by selecting exemplar loans and presenting those to a judge, arbitration panel, or jury for decision, the parties can apply those results to the remaining loans in dispute and work out their disputes without having to present every loan for a decision.

In addition to disputes regarding individual loans, there are certain fundamental disputes regarding how the mortgage insurance policies should be interpreted and applied to individual claim situations. In general, lenders and mortgage insurers dispute how the policies should be interpreted and applied, and getting resolutions of these disputes can be helpful to the parties in avoiding some disputes regarding coverage for individual mortgage loans.

The interpretation of insurance contracts is governed by state law. Under California law, for example, courts have held that insurance policies are subject to the ordinary rules of contract interpretation. Thus, the primary goal is to give effect to the mutual intent of the parties at the time of contracting. *MacKinnon v. Truck Ins. Exch.*, 31 Cal. 4th 635, 647 (Cal. 2003).

This intent is determined, where possible, solely from reviewing the terms of the contract, and if there is a clear and explicit meaning to be given to the contract, that meaning controls interpretation. *Id.* at 647-648.

Where policy language is ambiguous, courts generally construe the ambiguity against the drafter of the language, which, in the case of an insurance policy, is the insurance company. *Powerine Oil Co. v. Superior Court*, 37 Cal. 4th 377, 391 (Cal. 2005). Further, coverage provisions in a policy are interpreted broadly in favor of the policyholder, and exclusionary language is interpreted narrowly against the insured. It is the insurance company's burden to phrase exclusionary clauses in clear and unmistakable language. *MacKinnon*, 31 Cal. 4th 635. These general rules of insurance policy interpretation apply to mortgage insurance, like any other type of insurance. 660 F. Supp. 2d at 1175. Thus, to the extent that mortgage insurers seek to deny coverage based on exclusionary language in their policies, courts are instructed to construe that language narrowly against the insurers and in favor of coverage.

Challenges and Obstacles to an Effective Strategy and Litigation

While there have been disputes over the years between mortgage insurers and lenders, they have not been at the level that they are today. The number of claims involved is enormous, as are the financial stakes. The complexity of the cases and their high stakes create barriers. Parties trying to work together to structure the litigation in an effective way may encounter difficulties. While the policyholders want to have the cases resolved quickly so that they can get paid by the insurers, the insurers on the other hand have an incentive to drag things out to avoid payment for as long as possible. They also wish to avoid precedent-setting decisions that can be used by other insureds.

It will take strong case management by the courts or by arbitrators to move the cases toward efficient resolution and to develop creative solutions to the logistical challenges. In addition, the parties should attempt to collaborate to develop efficient means to bring cases to resolution. The use of alternative dispute resolution procedures should be considered, including the possibility of setting up fast and efficient mechanisms for resolving individual claims short of a full-blown trial or arbitration proceeding. One possible alternative is for the parties to agree to a panel of arbitrators to randomly hear and resolve disputes as to individual loans on an expedited and binding basis.

The Use of Experts during Litigation

Experts are an important part of litigation regarding mortgage fraud, including cases involving mortgage insurance disputes. Experts can and should be utilized in a number of areas. Where mortgage-backed securitizations are at issue, experts familiar with securitizations and how they were put together, rated, and marketed to investors can be useful. Because many of the issues in dispute revolve around how individual mortgages were underwritten and whether there was fraud or other improper conduct in the loan origination process, experts with hands-on mortgage underwriting experience can be critical. Experts in the appraisal industry also may be critical where appraisal issues are involved. In addition, experts knowledgeable about the mortgage insurance industry can be helpful to explain how insurers assess risk, evaluate loans, and handle claims. Where bad faith is alleged against an insurer, experts may be necessary to evaluate the insurance company's claims-handling practices to assess whether they were reasonable and complied with appropriate industry standards. Further, given the sheer volume of individual loans at issue in these cases, experts can be helpful in synthesizing and explaining large volumes of data to a court, jury, or arbitration panel.

Ultimately, the best experts are found by word-of-mouth through recommendations from colleagues and others handling similar claims. It is important to monitor litigation being handled by other attorneys to see which experts are being utilized and whether those experts are effective and credible. Ideally, individuals with hands-on experience in the different fields will make the best experts. People who have actually underwritten loans or handled claims at an insurance company will be the most effective and believable, provided they have the communication skills to impart their knowledge.

Conclusion

Even with the economic recovery under way, the number of mortgage loan defaults and foreclosures has not gone down, so there will continue to be large numbers of insurance claims and continued assertions of fraud by the mortgage insurers in an effort to hold down claim payments. Eventually, things will stabilize, and the numbers of claims will begin to taper off.

At the same time, in response to the financial crisis, lenders and insurers have tightened their underwriting guidelines and have eliminated certain risky mortgage products that have been the focus of much criticism. As we have learned from history, the mortgage industry is cyclical. In response to periods of financial distress, the marketplace tends to tighten, and guidelines become stricter. When the economy improves, the marketplace opens up, and guidelines are loosened. It will be interesting to see what happens to the mortgage market when the inevitable economic recovery takes place and housing prices stabilize and again start to rise. Whether we go back to more liberal practices remains to be seen.

Advice for Practitioners

Working in the insurance recovery field has always been fascinating because it usually exists on the cutting edge of the law. Whenever there is a major crisis in the news, insurance issues are implicated in one way or another.

Attorneys practicing in this field need to stay on top of current events and must have the ability to become experts quickly in almost every area of the law and business. One day you might be an expert regarding stock option practices to respond to issues arising from scandals relating to options backdating, and the next day you need to become an expert regarding mortgages and mortgage-backed securitizations. Then the next day it will be something completely different that you never expected. That is what makes this field interesting, and there is never a dull moment.

Attorneys new to the insurance recovery practice should take time to first learn the basics. There is general law governing insurance coverage disputes in every jurisdiction, and this law should be studied and mastered. There are good practice guides available and numerous seminars to attend. The American Bar Association has a section devoted entirely to insurance coverage issues. Once the basics are mastered, then the attorney can start to focus on specific subject areas.

Key Takeaways

• Many mortgage insurance policies have suit limitation provisions that generally run from the date a claim is denied. These need to be monitored so that rights are not lost.

• Exercise strong case management to bring policyholders and insurers together during litigation. The former are motivated by speed; the latter, by avoidance of payment and binding precedent.

• Use mortgage underwriting and appraisal experts to prove or disprove fraud or other improper conduct in the loan origination process.

• Consider the use of alternative dispute resolution procedures to resolve individual claims short of a full-blown trial or arbitration proceeding.

• Monitor litigation being handled by other attorneys to see which experts are being utilized and whether those experts are effective and credible.

• Stay on top of current events and news, and learn as much as possible about different areas of law and business. Insurance companies are implicated in nearly every business issue.

David E. Weiss is a partner in Reed Smith LLP's Litigation Insurance Recovery Group. He has represented corporate policyholders in complex insurance coverage disputes since 1990. He has represented clients in a wide variety of insurance matters, from high-stakes litigation to providing advice to policyholders with respect to the presentation of claims and the negotiation of settlements, including alternative dispute resolution. He also assists clients in their procurement of insurance, including the drafting and negotiation of policy language and the review and analysis of insurance policy forms, and he has assisted corporate clients in providing training to their personnel regarding various insurance issues.

Mr. Weiss has represented policyholder clients over the years in a wide variety of disputes under all types of insurance policies, including directors and officers liability insurance, errors and omissions liability insurance, commercial general liability insurance, crime insurance, first-party property insurance, business interruption insurance, fidelity insurance, employment practices liability insurance, and fiduciary liability insurance.

Mr. Weiss currently represents clients in mortgage insurance litigation, claims regarding stock option dating and other alleged securities violations, breach of fiduciary duties, interference with contract and prospective economic advantage, environmental liabilities, employee theft, computer crime, mortgage fraud, and wrongful termination.

Before joining Reed Smith LLP in 2007, Mr. Weiss was Morgan, Lewis & Bockius LLP, and prior to that, Brobeck, Phleger & Harrison LLP.

Mr. Weiss earned a J.D., cum laude, at the University of San Francisco School of Law, where he was a member of the McAuliffe Honor Society and a Law Review *staff member. He received his B.A. at the University of California, Berkeley.*

Protecting the Validity and Priority of Mortgage Liens in the Midst of Fraudulent Schemes

Michael R. O'Donnell

Partner

Riker Danzig Scherer Hyland & Perretti LLP

ASPATORE

Introduction

You have just been informed that a loan your institution has extended and that is secured by a mortgage is, in whole or part, the product of fraud. Is there any way you can preserve your mortgage? Yes. Even in situations where the putative borrower alleges that he or she did not give a mortgage, did not get value for the mortgage, or did not record the mortgage in a timely fashion, a lender may be able to protect the validity and priority of its mortgage under certain circumstances.

This chapter discusses five legal mechanisms by which a lender can defend the priority of its mortgage lien when faced with allegations of or actual fraud relating to the loan it made: equitable subrogation, ratification, reformation, equitable mortgage, and cure of defective notarization. Application of these equitable principles will aid mortgage lenders as they seek to mitigate losses due to fraud.

Equitable Subrogation

The doctrine of equitable subrogation holds the lender's mortgage may obtain priority over earlier-recorded mortgages or liens not discharged for some reason (usually mistake or fraud) if that lender's mortgage loan paid off liens that were themselves superior to the earlier-recorded liens not discharged. The doctrine is an exception to the well-established principle that the first-recorded lien still of record prevails. See e.g., N.J. STAT. ANN. 46:21-1 (West 2003); see also TENN. CODE ANN. §66-26-101 (West 2009). In sum, it is an "equitable remedy invoked to reorder the priorities so that the lien that was junior remains so, and the new lien obtains priority position to the amount of the lien it paid off." J. BUSHNELL NIELSEN, TITLE & ESCROW CLAIMS GUIDE, § 3.4.7.3 (Woodridge Legal Publishers, 2d ed. 2007); see also RESTATEMENT (THIRD) OF PROP. § 7.6 (1997) (discussing the general availability of equitable subrogation to a mortgagee that paid a prior lien as a result of fraud or mistake). See also, *Metrobank for Sav., FSB v. Nat'l Cmty. Bank of N.J.*, 620 A.2d 433, 438 (N.J. Super. Ct. App. Div. 1993); *Suntrust Bank v. Riverside Nat'l. Bank of Fla.*, 792 So. 2d 1222 (Fla. 4th Dist. Ct. App. 2001); *Smith v. State Sav. & Loan Ass'n.*, 175 Ca. App. 3d 1092 (Cal. 2d. Dist. Ct. App. 1985); *United States v. Baran*, 996

F.2d 25 (2nd Cir. 1993). (See Appendix A for a Sample Equitable Subrogation Pleading.)

While it may not always be applicable, a lender should evaluate invoking the doctrine of equitable subrogation whenever its loan funds have been used to pay off a prior lien. For example, equitable subrogation may apply where, because of fraudulent conduct, an intervening lien was not discharged as contemplated in connection with the loan transaction. The doctrine may also apply where a lender's lien was not recorded promptly, thereby causing it to lose its first-tier position. Finally, equitable subrogation does not apply just to the payment of prior mortgages, but also to "all kinds of debts," including the payment of real estate taxes. *See* NIELSEN, § 3.4.7.3.

When evaluating the application of equitable subrogation to a particular loan, a lender must focus on whether it was aware of the intervening lien over which it seeks to assert priority, and if not, why it was not. States differ as to whether a lender's knowledge of an intervening lien bars the use of equitable subrogation. In certain states, equitable subrogation does not apply when the lender seeking to assert the doctrine has actual knowledge of an intervening lien. See also, *Metrobank*, 620 A.2d at 439 ("a mortgagee who accepts a mortgage whose proceeds are used to pay off an old mortgage is subrogated to the extent of the loan only where the new mortgagee lacks knowledge of other encumbrances."). In others, the remedy of equitable subrogation is available even where the lender had actual knowledge of the intervening lien. See *Lamb Excavation Inc. v. Chase Manhattan Mortgage Corp.*, 95 P.3d 542, 544 (Ariz. 2004) (awarding equitable subrogation to lender who had actual notice of the intervening lien); *E. Sav. Bank, FSB v. Pappas*, 829 A.2d 953 (D.C. 2003).

States also differ as to the effect of the negligence of a lender or its agent in failing to discover an intervening lien. Some states hold that, even where the lack of knowledge is due to negligence on the part of the subsequent mortgagee, equitable subrogation may still be effective. *Metrobank*, 620 A.2d at 438-439; *Trus Joist Corp. v. Nat'l Union Fire Ins. Co.*, 462 A.2d 603, 609 (N.J. Super. Ct. App. Div. 1983) ("There is no doubt that a mortgagee who negligently accepts a mortgage without knowledge of intervening encumbrances will subrogate to a first mortgage with priority over the intervening encumbrances to the extent that the proceeds of the new mortgage are used to satisfy the old mortgage."), rev'd on other grounds sub nom, *Trus Joist Corp. v. Treetop Assocs. Inc.*, 477 A.2d 817 (N.J. 1984). Other states require a lender "to offer an excuse for his failure to discover the intervening lien." *See* NIELSON at § 3.4.7.3 (citing *Hieber v. Fla. Nat'l. Bank*, 522 So. 2d 878 (Fla. Dist. Ct. App. 1988) (denying equitable subrogation where purchaser missed junior lien, despite that it paid off another lien and the junior lien was of record)). Finally, certain states also preclude the use of equitable subrogation where the lender or its title insurer was negligent in performing the title search. See, e.g., *Roth v. Porush*, 281 A.D.2d 612 (N.Y. App. Div. 2001) (finding that equitable subrogation does not apply where title insurer missed intervening lien); *Centreville Car Care Inc. v. N. Am. Mortgage Co.*, 559 S.E.2d 870 (Va. 2002).

The application of equitable subrogation becomes more complex when a lender's loan funds have been used to pay down a first-position lien securing a line of credit. This is because most courts hold that the mere pay-off of a line of credit, unaccompanied by a signed authorization from the borrower to close the line, only pays down the lien but does not extinguish it. See, e.g., *First Union Nat'l Bank v. Nelkin*, 808 A.2d 856 (N.J. Super. Ct. App. Div. 2002) (denying equitable subrogation to a lender who paid off a line of credit where no signed authorization from the borrower was included.); *Chase Manhattan Bank v. Parker*, 2005 WL 880235 (Ohio Ct. App. Dist. Apr. 18, 2005). In such cases, the lien remains open, and the lender cannot be said to have discharged it.

Illustrating the Use of Equitable Subrogation: Sample Cases

Mortgage Electronic Registration Systems v. Massimo

An example of a lender's use of the doctrine of equitable subrogation to protect the priority of its mortgage is found in *Mortgage Ele.c Registration Sys., Inc. v. Massimo*. 2006 WL 1477125 at *1 (N.J. Super. Ct. App. Div. May 26, 2006). In *Massimo*, SIB Ivy Mortgage Corporation (SIB) sought a judicial determination that a mortgage given to it had priority over a mortgage in favor of a prior lender, Advantage Bank (Advantage). There, the borrower/owner Massimo first executed a note and mortgage in favor of SIB. He then mortgaged the same property to Advantage Bank. About a year later, Massimo asked Advantage for permission to refinance the existing SIB mortgage. Advantage agreed to the refinance and stated that it would discharge its mortgage and record a new mortgage once the refinanced mortgage was recorded. SIB funded the re-finance loan, and the bulk of these proceeds were used to pay off its existing mortgage loan. Massimo then defaulted on the notes and mortgages given to SIB and Advantage, and a foreclosure action ensued.

The court found that SIB's mortgage was entitled to priority on the grounds of equitable subrogation. In doing so, the court noted that Advantage specifically agreed to grant priority to the refinancing of SIB's mortgage. It further noted that SIB did not have actual knowledge of Advantage's second mortgage, as it was recorded just five days before SIB's refinance. Finally, the court further found that Advantage would be unjustly enriched if it were allowed to jump ahead of at least the amount owed on the SIB mortgage recorded first that was discharged per the refinance ($502,000).

United Orient Bank v. Lee

While the court did not specifically refer to equitable subrogation, it applied similar principles in *United Orient Bank v. Lee*, 504 A.2d 1215 (N.J. Super. Ct. App. Div. 1986). In *United Orient*, the borrower refinanced his home and used funds from the refinance to pay off a prior mortgage with United Orient Bank. The payoff was accompanied by a cover letter that stated that the check represented "payment in full for your mortgage/loan as above. Interest has been added through June 4, 1984." Moreover, the payoff check bore the notation "Lee refinance mtg payoff 636 Kenwood Rd., Ridgewood, N.J." However, despite the explicit instructions, United Orient Bank applied these proceeds to a different loan for which the mortgagor was a guarantor and commenced a foreclosure proceeding on the mortgage that the refinancing bank intended to pay off. The court held that the United Orient Bank mortgage should have been paid off, finding that "having accepted the check which was the subject to these limitations [set forth in the cover letter and noted on the check], plaintiff had an independent duty to carry out these instructions" and discharge the mortgage. Id. at 1218. The court further held that "[t]he deposit of the check with the instructions "constituted acceptance of these terms, and plaintiff thereafter had no right to act in derogation of defendants' directions." Id.

Centreville Car Care Inc. v. North American Mortgage Co.

Centreville Car Care Inc. v. North American Mortgage Co. represents a case where the doctrine of equitable subrogation was held not to apply. 559 S.E.2d 870 (Va. 2002). Fleet Mortgage Corporation (Fleet) was the holder of a first lien position on the relevant property, with Centreville Car Care Inc. (Centreville) holding a second lien position. When the property was sold, a new purchaser took out a loan from North American Mortgage Co. (North American) to make the purchase. North American paid off the Fleet loan; however, the title search missed the Centreville lien. Therefore, because of the sale, the Centreville lien got advanced to a first lien position, with North American assuming a second lien. North American then moved to be equitably subrogated to Fleet's first lien position.

In reversing the lower court, the Virginia Supreme Court found that the equities favored denying North American's request for equitable subrogation. Specifically, the court found that it was North American's negligence in failing to discover the Centreville mortgage in the first place. Moreover, North American could have a possible recovery for this negligence from either the title searcher or the title insurance company. Finally, the court found that, if North American were granted equitable subrogation, Centreville would be prejudiced in that the original owner of the home was still obligated under the promissory note, but the collateral no longer belonged to them. Therefore, there was no incentive for the original owner to pay the Centreville mortgage. The court thus found that the equities favored Centreville and denied North American's request for equitable subrogation.

Ratification

Ratification is the "affirmance by a person of a prior act which did not bind him but which was done, or professedly done on his account, whereby the act, as to some or all persons, is given effect as if originally authorized by him." RESTATEMENT (SECOND) OF AGENCY § 82 (1957). The doctrine makes it "possible for a principal to be bound by an unauthorized act of the agent by ratifying the agent's act." 10 THOMPSON ON REAL PROPERTY § 86.02(b)(4) (1998). Ratification is not a doctrine unique to property or lending law, but rather is a general principle of agency law. RESTATEMENT (SECOND) OF AGENCY § 82 (1957).

Some courts, including those in New Jersey, New York, Maryland, and Tennessee, have applied the doctrine of ratification to uphold the validity of mortgages in situations where a mortgage was fraudulently obtained in the name of a borrower, but the borrower later ratified the transaction. *Rothschild v. Title Guarantee & Trust Co.*, 97 N.E. 879 (N.Y. 1912) (A mortgagor who knew her signature was forged and paid two installments of interest on the mortgage could not protest the validity of the mortgage.); *Smith v. Merritt Sav. & Loan Inc.*, 295 A.2d 474, 480 (Md. 1972) (holding that while the original transaction was invalid, plaintiff had ratified the mortgage by retaining the benefits from the proceeds of the mortgage after he obtained knowledge of the transaction.); *Citizens First Nat'l Bank of N.J. v. Bluh*, 656 A.2d 853 (N.J. Super. Ct. App. Div. 1995); *Farmers' Loan & T. Co. v. Memphis & C. R. Co.*, 83 F. 870 (W.D. Tenn. 1897); *Jones v. Watkins*, 140 So. 920 (Fla. 1932). These cases stand for the proposition that a "defect in the execution of a mortgage may be cured by the subsequent act of the mortgagor in ratifying it and acknowledging its validity." 59 C.J.S. Mortgages § 160 (2010). Thus, a borrower "may ratify a mortgage to which his signature was forged, by receiving and appropriating the proceeds with full knowledge of the proceeds or by voluntarily paying interest on the mortgage." *Id.* (citing *Livings v. Wiler*, 32 Ill. 387 (1863); *Rothschild*, 97 N.E. at 879)).

It must be noted, however, that other cases have reached the opposite result, holding under facts that where a mortgage or deed of trust contains a forged signature by one not authorized to make it, it cannot be ratified by the borrower because the instrument is void as a matter of public policy. *See* 59 C.J.S. Mortgages § 160 (citing *1st Coppell Bank v. Smith* 742 S.W.2d 454 (Tex. App. 1987) (Deed of trust containing forged signatures cannot be validated by ratification); *Finley v. Babb*, 46 S.W. 165 (Mo. 1898) (mortgage to which mortgagor's name and acknowledgement were forged is void despite acquiescence and ratification by mortgagee)); *Henry*

Christian Bldg. & Loan Assoc. v. Walton, 37 A. 261 (Pa. 1897) ("forger does not act on behalf nor profess to represent person whose handwriting he counterfeits and the subsequent adoption of instrument cannot supply authority which forger did not profess to have"). While the applicability of the doctrine of ratification to a fraudulently obtained mortgage loan may vary depending on the facts and jurisdiction, a lender should analyze whether the doctrine applies whenever its borrower claims that she either did not sign or was fraudulently induced into signing the note and/or mortgage.

In states where a party can ratify a mortgage obtained by fraud, a lender must show that that the actions of the putative borrower demonstrate that the parties had full knowledge of the situation and intended to confirm the mortgage. C.J.S. Mortgages § 190 ("To ratify a mortgage procured by fraud, there must be an unequivocal act of confirmation made with full knowledge of the facts, and where one acts in ignorance of the true facts, ordinarily no ratification results."). The party to be charged must adopt the forgery or apparent signature as her own. 9-95 Warren's Weed New York Real Property § 95.24. ("A mortgage will, however, be later binding on the parties if the party to be charged subsequently adopts the forgery or apparent signature as the party's own signature with the intent thereby to authenticate the instrument."). Evidence of intent to adopt the fraudulently obtained mortgage can be found from the fact that the putative borrower knew of the fraud and sought to enforce the agreements (*Kepler v. Kepler*, 199 A. 198 (Pa. 1938)), accepted the benefits of the mortgage loan, paid interest thereon, and asked for a forbearance in making payments (*Carr v. McColgan*, 60 A. 606 (Md. 1905) (by accepting the benefit of the mortgage loan, paying interest, asking for forbearance, and participating in a mortgage sale without raising a claim of fraud, mortgagors were estopped from excepting the validity of the mortgage)) or utilized the funds loaned pursuant to the mortgage. (*DeAndrade v. Trans Union LLC*, 2006 WL 5671233 at *6 (D.R.I. Nov. 29, 2006) ("Plaintiff's use and enjoyment of the windows for twenty-two months and his utilization of Key Bank's money to pay for those windows establishes ratification of the agent's acts and acceptance of the Key Bank loan")).

Sample Ratification Cases

Citizens First National Bank of New Jersey v. Bluh

An example of a court applying the doctrine of ratification in favor of a mortgage lender can be found in *Citizens First Nat'l Bank of N.J. v. Bluh*, 656 A.2d 853 (N.J. Super. Ct. App. Div. 1995). In *Citizens*, a partnership owned a tract of land, and one of the partners, Cavaliere, mortgaged this property without the required approval of the partnership for a personal loan. The other partner, Bluh, learned that the mortgage had been entered without his consent. Despite the fact that he was aware that the mortgage executed by Cavaliere would have first priority and that the mortgage could be claimed to be invalid, he allegedly did nothing to enforce the rights of the partnership. Instead, he entered into a subsequent partnership agreement with Cavaliere and continued to use Cavaliere as his attorney in two of his other mortgage transactions. Bluh later sought to have the mortgage discharged. The trial court ruled the mortgage was void *ab initio*, as Cavaliere was not authorized to place the mortgage on the property.

The Appellate Court reversed, holding that the mortgage was not void *ab initio*, as Bluh may have ratified Cavaliere's actions in granting the mortgage by failing to repudiate the transaction upon learning of it. The court then remanded the case on this issue for a determination as to whether Bluh ratified the transaction, given his alleged acquiescence and participating in negotiating a new partnership agreement concerning the mortgage.

Espinosa v. Martin

Espinosa v. Martin provides a recent example of a how a court determined that the doctrine of ratification did not protect a bank. 520 S.E.2d 108, 111 (N.C. Ct. App. 1999), *cert. den.* 543 S.E.2d 126 (N.C. 2000). There, a bank brought action for foreclosure against putative mortgagors Cheri and Jamie Espinosa, who were deeded property from Ms. Espinosa's sister, but did not obtain a mortgage loan in connection with the transaction and disavowed making a mortgage. The trial court found that Cheri Espinosa's father forged their signatures and received the loan proceeds. In response to the putative mortgagors' claim that they did not sign the mortgage, the bank argued that the borrowers ratified the transaction by retaining the property after they learned of a forgery. The court held that the borrowers did not ratify the transaction because there was no evidence that they received the loan proceeds or that they had knowledge of the loan transaction.

Reformation and Recording *Nunc pro Tunc*

The doctrine of reformation applies when parties intend to form a contract, but "the resulting writing does not accurately reflect the intention of the parties." See 7 CORBIN ON CONTRACTS § 28.45 (1998). The purpose of the doctrine is to allow a contract to be reformed so that "[t]he reformed [document] corrects the language used so that it reads as it should have read all along." 14 POWELL ON REAL PROPERTY, § 901[3] (1998). Reformation of a contract cannot modify the intention of the parties. See *Lederman v. Prudential Life Ins. Co. of Am. Inc.*, 897 A.2d 373, 385 (N.J. Super. Ct. App. Div. 2006). "The reformation of an instrument relates back to the time the instrument was originally executed and simply corrects the document's language to read as the instrument should have read all along." 66 AM. JUR. 2D *Reformation of Instruments* § 9 (2010).

Although specific standards vary from state to state, broadly stated, the "grounds for the reformation of an instrument are generally limited to: (1) mistake; or (2) fraudulent or inequitable conduct." 66 AM. JUR. 2D *Reformation of Instruments* § 10 (2010); see also 76 C.J.S. *Reformation of Instruments* § 25 (2010) ("It has thus been recognized that "relief will be granted without regard to the cause of the failure to express the contract as actually made of the intent of the parties, whether due to fraud, mistake in the use of the language or any other thing which prevented the expression of the true intention of the parties, and that if by reason of fraud, inequitable conduct, mistake, inadvertence accident or surprise the instrument fails to express the true intent and meaning of the parties, equity will on satisfactory evidence reform it."); *St. Pius X House of Retreats, Salvatorian Fathers v. Diocese of Camden*, 443 A.2d 1052, 1055 (N.J. 1982) ("The traditional grounds justifying reformation of an instrument are either mutual mistake or unilateral mistake by one party and fraud or unconscionable conduct by the other.").

When seeking to reform a document based on mistake, it generally must be established that the mistake is mutual by both parties. *See id.*; *Matter of Enstar Corp.*, 604 A.2d 404 (Del. 1992). Where fraud or inequitable conduct is established, a mutual mistake by the parties need not be shown. When seeking to obtain reformation based on fraud, however, it must generally be established that a party made a material representation or concealed a material fact on which the other party relied. See 66 AM. JUR. 2D *Reformation of Instruments* §§ 23-24.

The doctrine of reformation has been repeatedly held to apply to deeds by states across the country. See 66 AM. JUR. 2D *Reformation of Instruments* § 30 (citing *Palmer v. Palmer*, 390 So. 2d 1050 (Ala. 1980); *City of Fargo v. D.T.L. Props. Inc.*, 564 N.W.2d 274 (N.D. 1997); *O'Donnell v. O'Donnell*, 202 S.W.2d 999 (Ky. Ct. App. 1947); *Fisher v. Standard Inv. Co.*, 15 N.W.2d 355 (Neb. 1944)). It has also been widely applied to mortgages. *See id.* (citing *Sunshine Bank of Ft. Walton Beach v. Smith*, 631 So. 2d 965 (Ala. 1994); *Grappo v. Mauch*, 110 Nev. 1396 (1994); *Hopkins v. Mills*, 156 So. 532 (Fla. 1934); *Bruenn v. Switlik*, 447 A.2d 583 (N.J. Super. Ct. App. Div. 1982); *Busey v. Moraga*, 62 P. 1081 (Cal. 1900); *Thompson v. Estate of Coffield*, 894 P.2d 1065 (Okla. 1995)). A lender who is faced with loan fraud should carefully determine whether it could preserve the validity of its mortgage or deed by relying on the doctrine of reformation. Situations in which reformation may be able to aid a lender include those in which a borrower involved in a fraud attempts to disclaim responsibility based on technicalities in the documents.

Sample Cases Showing Reformation in Action

Sunshine Bank of Fort Walton Beach v. Smith

In *Sunshine Bank of Fort Walton Beach v. Smith*, defendant lent a third party, Kemp, $56,000 to purchase certain real property. 631 So. 2d 965 (Ala. 1994). In exchange, Kemp obtained a purchase-money mortgage on the property. However, because of a scrivener's error, the mortgage listed the incorrect address of the property, instead containing the neighbor's address. Thereafter, plaintiff obtained a judgment against Kemp. The court ultimately permitted reformation of the mortgage to gain priority over plaintiff's judgment where "the clear intention, as manifested by all the parties to the contract and the mortgage, was that Kemp purchase the real estate [with the correct address], and that [defendant] provide the purchase money and receive in return a purchase money mortgage covering that real property."

Holiday Hospitality Franchising Inc. v. State Resources Inc

Holiday Hospitality Franchising Inc. v. State Res. Inc. provides another illustrative case of the application of the doctrine of reformation. 232 S.W.3d 41 (Tenn. Ct. App. 2006). There, the Tennessee Court of Appeals evaluated the competing interests in restoring a mortgage lien, which had mistakenly been discharged, and the priority of intervening judgment creditors. Tennessee is a "race notice" state. *See* TENN. CODE ANN. §66-26-101 (West 2010). *Nunc pro tunc* recordation was granted. In *Holiday*, a developer secured a construction loan to improve two lots, 13 and 30. The lender recorded the mortgage, which encompassed both lots. After the completion of construction of lot 13, the developer sold it and used the proceeds to pay off a portion of the mortgage. The original mortgage, which encompassed both lots, was still unsatisfied, and the lender should have maintained a recorded lien on lot 30. After the closing, however, the lender recorded a release of both. The conveyance of the deed to lot 13 from the developer to a third-party purchaser was then recorded. After recording the release, two judgments were entered against the developer and entered as liens against lot 30. The lender petitioned the court and argued that: (1) an erroneous release had been executed and filed because of mutual mistake; (2) the judgment creditor did not rely on the recorded title information in asserting its judgment lien; and (3) equitable principles justified a reformation of the release to reinstate the original deed of trust.

The *Holiday* court permitted a corrective filing canceling the erroneous release. It reasoned that the release or satisfaction of a mortgage resulting from fraud should not benefit a party that acquired an interest in the property but did not rely on the notice of discharge. Because a judgment lien creditor has no duty to inspect title records, its rights will not ordinarily preclude relief sought by a deed holder. The court noted that the judgment lienor's interest attaches upon the filing of the judgment and that record notice does not affect the lienor's rights. Id.; see also *Sunshine Bank*, 631 So. 2d at 968. (finding that where purchase money mortgage is reformed, the judgment creditor is in no worse place than it would have been had the mortgage been recorded with the correct address). Thus, the restoration of a mortgage to its priority of lien does not place the judgment creditor in a worse position than he should have been in. The court concluded that it was equitable to balance the "benefit of absolution from record notice with the risk of deed reinstatement," where such restoration places the judgment lien creditor in no worse position. *See Holiday*, 232 S.W.3d at 53.

Once a deed or mortgage has been reformed to protect a lender's lien status, the lender should seek to have the instrument recorded *nunc pro tunc*. Recordation *nunc pro tunc* refers to the recording of a reformed instrument at the direction of a court designed to correct a previously recorded incorrect instrument. BLACK'S LAW DICTIONARY (6th ed. 1991); *In re Marriage of Hirsch*, 482 N.E.2d 625, 632 (Ill. App. Ct. 1985) ("nunc pro tunc order is an entry now for something previously done, made to make the record speak now for what was actually done then"). When a reformed document is recorded *nunc pro tunc*, the effective date of its recording is the date of recordation of the original instrument.

Equitable Lien/Equitable Mortgage

Another equitable tool on which a lender can rely if it does not have a valid mortgage because of fraud is that of the doctrine of equitable lien/ mortgage. (See Appendix B for a Sample Equitable Lien/Mortgage and Reformation Nunc pro Tunc Pleading.) "An equitable lien is the right to have property subjected, in a court of equity, to the payment of a claim. It is neither a debt nor a right of property but a remedy for a debt. It is simply a right of a special nature over the property which constitutes a charge or encumbrance thereon....." *Hargrove v. Gerill Corp.*, 464 N.E.2d 1226, 1231 (Ill. App. Ct. 1984) (quotation omitted) (cited by 59 CJ.S. *Mortgages* § 12). An equitable mortgage is a specific type of equitable lien created "where money is loaned or credit given in reliance upon the security of property of the debtor, but pledged by him in such manner as not to be enforceable as a mortgage at law." *Id.* at 1230; *Hamilton Trust Co. v. Clemes*, 57 N.E. 614 (N.Y. 1900) ("'an equitable mortgage may be constituted by any writing from which the intention so to do may be gathered, and an attempt to make a legal mortgage, which fails for the want of some solemnity, is valid in equity; ... a specific lien upon the land, ... and that an equitable mortgage thus created is entitled to a preference over subsequent judgment creditors.'"); see also *FDIC v. Five Star Mgmt. Inc.*, 258 A.D.2d 15, 21 (N.Y. App. Div. Jun. 17, 1999). 4 *Pomeroy's Equity Jurisprudence* § 1235 at 696 (5th ed. 1941) ("An equitable lien may be imposed where there exists an agreement in which: the contracting party sufficiently indicates an intention to make some particular property, real or personal, or fund, therein described or identified, a security for a debt or other obligation, or whereby the party promises to convey or assign or transfer the property as security …"). When the transaction is the lending of money, to be secured by a mortgage, but the "mortgage …. is so defective or informal, as to fail in effectuating the purpose of its execution, equity will impress upon the land … a lien in favor of the creditor." *Sprague v. Cochran*, 38 N.E. 1000 (N.Y. 1894). The equitable lien arises from the loan, rather than from the formality of the instrument, and it continues in effect until satisfied or waived. 258 A.D.2d at 21.

Courts across the country have recognized the existence of equitable mortgages where parties intend to create a mortgage or lien on a property. *Boyarsky v. Froccaro*, 125 Misc. 2d 352 (N.Y. Sup. Ct. 1984); *Holmes v. Dunning*, 133 So. 557 (Fla. 1931). The essential element is the intent by the parties to create a lien on specific property. 59 C.J.S. *Mortgages* § 12. Significantly, the form of agreement that creates an equitable lien or mortgage is not dispositive because equity looks at the intent and purpose. "If an intent to give, charge or pledge property, real or personal, as security for an obligation appears, and the property or thing intended to be given, charged or pledged is sufficiently described or identified, then the equitable lien … will follow as of course." *Rutherford Nat'l Bank v. H.R. Bogle & Co.*, 169 A. 180, 182 (N.J. Super. Ct. Ch. Div. 1933); see also *Ulrich v. Ulrich*, 1 N.Y.S. 777 (N.Y. App. Div. 1888) (enforcing an equitable mortgage against a wife's interest in land that husband's actions created an equitable mortgage.); *In re Loring*, 301 A.2d 721, 723 (N.J. 1973) (assertion of attorney's equitable lien for a fee claim out of sale proceeds of house); *Cohen v. Estate of Sheridan*, 528 A.2d 101, 104 (N.J. Super. Ct. Ch. Div 1987) (real estate brokers have equitable lien for their commissions on proceeds of sale due vendor at closing). That said, it is important to realize that most courts hold that, in light of the statutes of fraud on agreements, the pledge to give a mortgage must be in writing to constitute an equitable mortgage. 59 C.J.S. *Mortgages* § 48.

"While the terms 'equitable lien' and 'equitable mortgage' are closely related, equitable lien is a more inclusive term than equitable mortgage, which in all instances requires an affirmative pledge of property as security for a debt." 59 C.J.S. *Mortgages* § 32. Often courts will use the two terms interchangeably. *Id.* (citing *Red River State Bank v. Reirson*, 533 N.W.2d 683 (N.D. 1995)). Both concepts arise from the well-settled maxim that "equity regards as done that which ought to be done. ..." *Hadley v. Passaic Nat'l Bank & Trust Co.*, 168 A. 38, 40 (N.J. Super. Ct. Ch. Div. 1933).

An equitable mortgage can be enforced between the original parties to the transaction or against a third party who has notice thereof. *See* 59 C.J.S. *Mortgages* § 51 (citing *Owens v. Cont'l Supply Co.*, 71 F.2d 862, 863 (10th Cir. 1934) ("Equity treats that as done which ought to be done. A valid agreement to execute a mortgage will be enforced in equity against the maker or third persons who have notice thereof, or who are volunteers."). An equitable mortgage can also be enforced against a person or entity who obtains an interest only by operation of law and not for valuable consideration. *See* 1 N.Y.S. 777 (enforcing an equitable mortgage against a wife's interest in land that husband's actions created an equitable mortgage.).

The ability to impose equitable liens and mortgages on property can be a valuable tool for lenders who have been defrauded—especially when the lender does not have a valid mortgage on which it can rely. Lenders who have been defrauded in connection with transactions involving real property can claim to have an equitable lien on all property held by those who have defrauded it. Moreover, in situations where a putative borrower agreed to make a lien on a particular property for the lender's benefit, the lender can seek to impose an equitable mortgage on the property.

Demonstrating Equitable Mortgage: F.D.I.C. v. Five Star Management Inc.

An illustrative case of the application of an equitable mortgage is *F.D.I.C. v. Five Star Management Inc.*, 258 A.D.2d 15 (N.Y. App. Div.1999). In *Five Star*, plaintiff was seeking to foreclose on a mortgage that was in default. The defendant debtor, however, asserted an affirmative defense that the mortgage was a nullity insofar as there was a scrivener's error in the deed conveying the premises to the mortgagee. Defendant moved for summary judgment on these grounds and the plaintiff cross-moved seeking, among other things, an equitable mortgage. In reversing the trial court, the Appellate Division granted summary judgment in favor of the plaintiff for an equitable mortgage, finding that "[t]he documentary evidence in this case, notwithstanding a glitch in a deed, sufficiently establishes the existence of the loan, the intent that it be secured by certain premises, and [defendant's] obligation … to satisfy the debt by a date certain." The court therefore permitted the plaintiff to foreclose on the property.

Notary Curative Statutes

Often the mortgage documents executed in connection with a fraudulent transaction have not been acknowledged properly, rendering them invalid under state law. See *In re Buckholz*, 224 B.R. 13, 23 (Bankr. D.N.J. 1998) (finding that mortgage that was not properly acknowledged because of a false notarization was not sufficient to perfect mortgagee's interest as to a subsequent bona fide purchaser for value). Many states, however, have curative provisions rendering improperly acknowledged mortgage instruments valid under certain circumstances. In particular, certain states provide that if a document has been recorded for a certain period of time, even if the acknowledgment is defective, it will still serve as notice to any subsequent bona fide purchaser for value. For example, in New Jersey, N.J. STAT. ANN. § 46:21-2 (West 2003), provides in relevant part that:

> When any deed or instrument of the nature or description set forth in section 46:16-1 of this title shall, for a period of six years or more, have stood on record in any of the lawful books of record in this state appropriate for such deed or instrument, the record of such deed or instrument shall, after the lapse of such period, be and become valid for every purpose of notice as provided by section 46:21-1 of this title, and such deed or instrument, the record and certified copy thereof, shall be received in evidence in every court and be as effectual as if the original deed or instrument had been produced and proved, notwithstanding the absence of, or any informality, defect, imperfection or uncertainty in, the acknowledgment or proof or the certificates thereof, but only when such deed or instrument shall be corroborated by evidence of

corresponding enjoyment or other equivalent or explanatory proof.

Similarly, California has a curative statute providing that a document that has been recorded for one year or more serves as notice to a subsequent purchaser for value despite a defect in the acknowledgment. *See* CAL. CIV. CODE § 1207 (West 2007) ("Any instrument affecting the title to real property, one year after the same has been copied into the proper book of record, kept in the office of any county recorder, imparts notice of its contents to subsequent purchasers and encumbrancers, notwithstanding any defect, omission, or informality in the execution of the instrument, or in the certificate of acknowledgment thereof, or the absence of any such certificate; but nothing herein affects the rights of purchasers or encumbrancers previous to the taking effect of this act."). Florida has a similar law curing a defective acknowledgment where an instrument has been recorded for at least seven years. *See* FLA. STAT. ANN. § 694.08 (West 2010). These statutes, however, "cannot apply to change rights that have vested in innocent purchasers for value before the act went into effect." 2 PATTON AND PALOMAR ON LAND TITLES § 366 (3d. ed. 2009).

Lenders should be familiar with the curative statutes of the states in which they do business. In states where such curative statutes exist, a lender may sustain its priority despite a defective acknowledgment, as long as the statutorily required time period has elapsed.

Conclusion

The legal tools discussed above are powerful tools lenders have to maintain the priority of their liens even when undisputed fraud has occurred. Lenders should be familiar with the specific provisions of the laws and case law in the states in which they do business regarding these topics. Thus, when faced with a mortgage fraud scheme, the lender should not automatically assume that its lien is void. Instead, a thorough factual and legal analysis must be conducted as to: (1) how the lender's loan benefited others as to enhancing their priority position; (2) the benefit conveyed to the borrower from the loan; (3) the borrower's actions during and after the fraud was uncovered or known to him; and (4) whether their state has any curative statutes applicable to their situation.

Michael R. O'Donnell is a partner at Riker Danzig Scherer Hyland & Perretti LLP and specializes in representing title companies and financial institutions in a variety of disputes. He has handled mortgage fraud claims ranging from claims in hundreds of thousands of dollars to those in excess of $30 million.

Acknowledgment: *I would like to extend my appreciation and thanks to Ronald Ahrens and Jonathan Sandler, associates at Riker Danzig Scherer Hyland & Perretti LLP, who provided invaluable assistance in researching and writing this chapter and without whom this chapter would not have been possible.*

Successful Strategies for Mortgage Fraud Litigation

Steven Martin Aaron

Partner

Husch Blackwell Sanders LLP

ASPATORE

Introduction

My white collar and civil litigation practice has a strong emphasis on mortgage fraud, with cases pending in state and federal courts. I am a former state prosecutor, and over the last three years, I have tried seven mortgage fraud cases. Four have resulted in complete defense verdicts for my client; two trials ended in split verdicts between plaintiff and client; and one resulted in a mistrial. Because of this experience, in both the civil and the criminal contexts, I have developed a unique perspective of the risks facing companies and individuals in the mortgage industry.

Recent Experience in Mortgage Litigation

Our most recent cases were a series of lawsuits that centered on what we refer to as "reverse mortgage fraud." The traditional notion of mortgage fraud is a mortgage company being defrauded by real estate agents, appraisers, purchasers, and/or mortgage brokers. However, these civil matters all concerned a specific homeowner/plaintiff who claimed he or she was defrauded by the mortgage broker—essentially, fraud committed within the context of a mortgage transaction, not fraud committed on a mortgage company. The general fact pattern for the series of cases in which we represented the mortgage lender is as follows:

Plaintiff entered into a contract with a home builder for various items of home remodeling. To pay for the remodeling, plaintiff subsequently sought a home equity loan, which allowed her to consolidate her debts, receive cash back, and pay for the remodeling. As required by the loan, an appraisal company performed an appraisal of the property. Plaintiff was approved for and received a loan that included payout at closing to the builder of an amount in excess of the original remodeling contract. After closing, the builder provided a check, in the amount of the difference between the original construction contract and the amount indicated on the HUD, to the loan originators. Plaintiff alleged a conspiracy among the builder, the appraiser, and the client lender in that the appraiser inflated the value of the home, which provided for a larger loan for plaintiff, to pay for the remodeling and to fund the alleged "kickback," and the larger loan increased the fees earned by client lender.

At first, this alleged conduct seems to fall within prohibited conduct within the Real Estate Settlement Procedures Act, 12 U.S.C. § 2601 (2010). (RESPA), which is an industry statute that must be followed on all loans and real estate transactions. However, RESPA is not, as we argued, applicable because the amount of the payout to the contractor was clearly disclosed on the Settlement Statement; the alleged kickback was not in exchange for settlement services; and the payout to the contractor is not, in and of itself, payment for settlement services. We argued that the homeowners got exactly what they wanted—a loan for remodeling and debt consolidation—but they were angry because the contractor performed poorly. In essence, they were trying to hold the mortgage company liable for loaning them money to pay for something they didn't like.

Anticipated Future Litigation

In the future, we expect to see more criminal matters regarding fraud in loan modifications and foreclosure assistance schemes and civil matters seeking buybacks as a result of the economic turmoil caused by defaults in mortgage loans. After the loan is closed, sold, and securitized, companies are trying to take advantage of the buyback provisions in the loan documents because the loans that are contained within the securitized mortgages are going into default. The parties who invested in mortgage-backed securities are now losing money on them because homeowners cannot afford their mortgages. The response is to "sue back" to the mortgage broker or whomever they can find that is still in existence in the succession of the sale of the securitized mortgages. Their claim is that something is wrong with the loan documents or the processing of the loan itself, when in actuality the companies are losing money because they are holding securitized mortgages that are not worth the paper they are written on.

Consumer Borrowing

Nationally borrowers are finding themselves in loans they cannot afford because they did not have the financial means before they entered into their loan agreement, or because the value of their loans is such that it does not make sense to continue paying mortgages when their property is worth less than the remaining balance. Borrowers are looking for ways to get out of their loans and for people they can blame. The ultimate question is who bears the responsibility for bad loans. Borrowers are trying to assert that it is the lending institutions' or mortgage brokers' responsibility to determine what they can and cannot afford. In other words, if the consumer is getting into a loan that does not make good economic sense, he or she feels it is the lender's duty to advise him or her of that fact.

Banks and brokers are responding that this approach turns responsibility on its head. A borrower has to take some personal responsibility for entering into a transaction that he or she believes is in his or her best interest. Lenders are not financial advisers. For most people, mortgages are the biggest financial transaction in which they will ever engage, and they should behave no differently than they do when contemplating or managing a 401(k) plan or some other type of long-term financial planning.

Borrowers must take responsibility for those transactions. In the next two to three years, this will be an interesting area of law because lenders and borrowers will be pointing fingers and trying to assign blame for ill-advised financial transactions. People suggest that the mortgage crisis was a result of big money and big banks and that everyone was trying to get rich.

Conversely, we believe the consumers bear responsibility in the whole debacle, as well. They wanted something, they got it, and now that there are problems with it, they blame someone else. If a consumer wants to buy an expensive car, it is not the duty of the dealership to ask, "Shouldn't you save some money for your children's college education?" Mortgage lenders should have no more responsibility to consumers than any other lenders for providing financial advice and determining what a consumer should do with his or her money.

Public Perception and the Effect on the Mortgage Industry

Consumers are looking to get out of deals that are of no further financial advantage to them. Suing lenders is one way to do this. The mortgage industry has taken a hit from a public perspective standpoint because the public believes the latest mortgage crunch is entirely generated by the mortgage industry itself. There is little sentiment that consumers wanted to capitalize on what they thought was a rapidly inflated holdout. Now that these holdouts are declining at a significant rate, they are looking for ways to try to get out of the transactions by arguing that they did not appreciate the risks getting in.

The Economic Crisis and Its Effect on Mortgage Fraud Claims

One interesting aspect of the crisis is the development of more and more "short sales." Short sales occur when someone has a home that was purchased at a good value, with a mortgage he or she can afford, but then because of the declining value of homes, they get "upside-down" on their mortgage. In other words, they owe more than the house is worth. As a result, the individuals do not want to keep paying on that mortgage. However, values will come back and will appreciate even more. The consumer may be upside-down on paper, but in five to ten years when the market rebounds, he or she will be in a good position again. However, some of the loans that fall into this situation had good interest rates, but because of job loss or other changes in financial circumstances, homeowners are at risk for default. They cannot hold on until the market returns, and they simply want out.

This puts the bank in an interesting situation. In a short sale, the bank accepts less than the full payoff of the loan, relieves the consumer of the debt, and minimizes the amount it will lose. Lending institutions are not entirely free of liability in this type of situation. The trend that saw lenders bundle mortgages together into mortgage-backed securities and sell off the package whet the appetite of the industry for more. That increased mortgage lending, and because the loans were bundled, the risk was spread across more loans. As a result, lenders became more lax in their standards to keep up with the demand for loans and had a compelling incentive to write increasingly risky loans. Nonetheless, short sales allow both consumer and lender to minimize loss and share the burden of responsibility.

The more aggressive a lender gets with lending, the more issues there are to spring out of nowhere. For the past three or four decades, Americans have been living on the edge of their financial means and spending more of their discretionary income. When there are economic downturns they are less likely to be able to withstand being laid off or unemployed for a significant amount of time. Less savings and loss of a job affect the ability to make a mortgage payment when it is affordable. A mortgage payment that was predicated on unrealistic expectations can be worse, and can make for a disastrous real estate market. The irony is that in these buyback situations, when big banks receive funds from the government bailout, the government may be coming after the bank for money that was intended to fix the problem.

Federal and State Regulations on Mortgage and Finance Fraud

We have seen an uptick in the inclination of the federal government to regulate the loan application process and the services provided in conjunction with the loans. The government has a tendency, when it notices a problem, to try to regulate every portion of a transaction. My opinion is that the mortgage meltdown and attendant problems are not something that can be regulated with statutes. These are fraud cases: the essential question is whether a person can afford something. No amount of regulation, unless there are objective criteria placed on lending that develop some ratio of income to expenses, is going to control this. I do not think that the federal government should regulate what kind of loans people can assume. It is appropriate for the government to develop safeguards, which they have done, but the primary problem lies in whether people can ultimately afford loans—not whether the technical components of the loans have been done correctly.

Department of Justice Initiatives

The Obama Administration has requested about $96 million for the Department of Justice's (DOJ) Fiscal Year 2011 budget to combat financial fraud, including mortgage fraud. DOJ has hired additional agents, prosecutors, litigators, and bankruptcy attorneys to aggressively pursue law enforcement and litigation activities, including mortgage fraud. Recently, U.S. Attorney General Eric Holder announced that DOJ was moving forward with more than 2,800 mortgage fraud cases, an increase of 400 percent from five years ago.

Treasury Department Enforcement

Federal Crimes Enforcement, a unit of the U.S. Treasury Department, filed a report stating that there have been about 15,000 Suspicious Activity

Reports (SARs) filed regarding fraudulent activity this year. The Bank Secrecy Act requires banks to file a SAR with the Financial Crimes Enforcement Network when they identify or suspect fraud. This represents about an 8 percent increase from the prior year.

Not all of the SAR activity indicates there was actual fraud, but it does indicate fraud is on the radar. Because of what happened during the mortgage crisis over the past two years, we will see many loan modifications, foreclosures, and scams. People will try to do loan modifications and assist people, and those activities will result in foreclosure fraud. There is the potential that someone who has already been defrauded in the mortgage crisis could fall victim to fraud a second time.

Challenges Facing Mortgage Brokers

The challenge facing mortgage brokers is less about legal standards and more about the public perception of the entire industry. What is perceived to be predatory lending is, in many cases, giving people money they have no right receiving. That is the biggest problem the industry has to overcome.

On the legal side, there is a standard: the industry has incentivized brokers to close transactions. The perception from the public is that loan originators will tell potential borrowers anything they want to hear if that will help them close the transaction. A juror's natural tendency is to disbelieve what an originator says and believe anything the borrower says to overcome the written documentation associated with the loan.

Strategies for Defending Mortgage Brokers

Our litigation strategy is straightforward: look at the loan documents and determine whether they fall within accepted industry standards; for example, debt-to-income ratios, loan-to-value ratios, and interest rates. If all of the industry ratios and standards are met, it is easier to defend mortgage brokers and companies because the actual documents reflect a proper transaction. If you can prove this, the defendant is in better shape, and the case reverts to a he-said-she-said scenario. The defense has to overcome the issues we spoke about earlier, such as public perception, in either a civil or a criminal context. When the loan documents are not in order and there is nothing to back up your defense, refute the government, or counter the plaintiff's claims, it is a difficult situation because of the public perception that exists about mortgage brokers.

Managing Costs of Litigation

Mortgage brokers need experienced trial lawyers who have tried similar cases and know what issues will incite a jury. Experienced attorneys are able to render more value by doing quality work in less time. Litigators must know the loan process and loan documents.

Companies can proactively counter legal action by instituting a compliance plan that detects and deters wrongful conduct. A compliance initiative requires buy-in from all members of the company to do things the right way. It also requires that the compliance program become a living and breathing document. Having a compliance plan that is not put into action can actually cause more problems. It shows that the company knew what needed to be done, but failed to do it. In other words, it is easier to prove that the act of wrongdoing was intentional. A company may have an attorney work with it on a compliance program, and that will cost some money, but the company can manage the program internally with a compliance officer and other individuals. Doing things the right way can save money before a lawsuit is filed or judgments are handed down.

Developing Strategy to Counter Fraud Claims

The first goal is to identify the transaction and ascertain, from a technical standpoint, that the loan originator acquired the proper information, had appropriate paperwork, and submitted a loan that was an accurate representation of the borrower's debt at the time they applied. That is the most critical factor in our cases.

One of the biggest obstacles to an effective strategy is of the heavy turnover in the industry. Mortgage originators come and go, and are hard to find after they leave for another job. Their memory about the details of a transaction is not clear. That becomes a real obstacle because it gives the impression that these people are not entirely competent or qualified.

Many different pieces of the puzzle form a real estate loan transaction: loan originators, mortgage brokers, buyers. When one entity is handling all the parts of a transaction, it is more transparent, and both sides are able to determine whether things are being done correctly. In fact, most transactions are handled by a variety of providers, and that makes litigation strategy challenging because if the client did not perform every part of the transaction without an error, it is sometimes difficult to overcome. Transparency is easier with a single entity handling the transaction.

Best Practices for Winning Mortgage Lawsuit Cases

A key to winning in a mortgage lawsuit case is developing credibility with the jurors and arguing the case effectively. Finding the right defenses and theories is necessary to argue a case properly, and overcoming the negative perception of mortgage companies is essential. Jurors must think of a mortgage transaction as a contract or a transaction between a consumer and a company. By taking the case out of the context of an emotionally charged, media-fueled issue, the case is about the facts. This strategy helps you be successful at trial. Even if the jury thinks otherwise, making the mortgage nothing more than a contractual agreement between a consumer and a company helps minimize the damages because it takes the emotion out of the case.

The most challenging aspect of a case for jurors is who should bear responsibility when loans go bad. They have a tendency to identify with consumers because they are consumers themselves. Jurors do not want to have someone's life destroyed because they entered into a bad transaction. This is the most difficult factual aspect of the case with which they must deal: holding the borrower responsible for his or her own acts.

Settling Cases

Settling these cases becomes a difficult proposition. Mortgage companies and brokers must defend themselves to avoid a rash of litigation. That causes costs to mount rapidly. Ultimately, the company must go to trial, which gets expensive for both sides. However, that cost can be used as an inducement to settle the case. While clients believe they must try each case, they also do not want to spend the time, hassle, and cost of trying a lawsuit.

Settling must be considered on a case-by-case basis, but you do not want to set a trend and spend all your time settling lawsuits as a cost of doing business. We were able to defend our cases because our loans were good, and we were able to overcome what the plaintiff had to say and how the evidence came in. However, if a plaintiff evokes sympathy because of age, income, education, or inexperience in commercial transactions, the jury sees the individual as vulnerable. That makes it more difficult for the mortgage company to be successful because jurors assign more liability to the lender and expect it to take a greater advisory role in a transaction when you have a vulnerable borrower.

The irony: loan documents contain disclosures that prohibit lenders from discriminating against an individual because of his or her education, sex, or race. The lender gets into trouble with the jury because the jury thinks the lender is taking advantage of the person. Ironically, if the mortgage company did not follow through with the process, it would be sued by the homeowner for discrimination.

Advice for Practitioners

Through the end of 2010 and into 2011, foreclosure and loan modification fraud cases will continue to increase. In addition, loan schemes that existed in the past will be investigated and subject to either civil or criminal charges for conduct that occurred one to two years ago. Buybacks for securitized mortgages will be a continuing phenomenon because companies that purchased bulk mortgage securities are now seeing several of those loans going into default. Regardless of whether these defaults were the product of fraud, companies that purchased these mortgage securities are bringing suit against any company that is still in existence in the chain of the purchase of the paper.

Therefore, understand your clients' business model, practices, and what they are trying to accomplish. Make sure these goals also allow the client to take steps to ensure that its customers and borrowers receive excellent service and are adequately protected from fraud in the industry. Be familiar with and make changes to the client's compliance plan to make sure the client itself effectively protects its interests during the entire loan transaction.

Many different entities are involved in a loan on the lending side. It is incumbent on the attorney to know the specific processes that his or her client utilizes to proactively provide advice and to adequately defend if litigation arises.

Steven Martin Aaron, a partner with Husch Blackwell Sanders LLP, focuses on the practice areas of business litigation; government compliance, investigations, and litigation; and white-collar criminal defense. Having conducted more than forty-five civil and criminal jury trials, he has achieved major trial victories in cases involving claims of mortgage fraud and inflated appraisals in conspiracy with mortgage brokers and others to defraud homeowners in mortgage transactions.

Mr. Aaron joined the law firm as an associate in 1998 and was named partner in 2003. Before joining the firm, he was assistant prosecuting attorney for Jackson County, Missouri, from 1993 to 1998.

A member of the American Bar Association and the Kansas City Metropolitan Bar Association, Mr. Aaron also serves as a member of the Steve Palermo Endowment for Spinal Cord Injury Research and the National Sports Center for the Disabled.

Mr. Aaron received a J.D. from the University of Missouri at Kansas City and a B.G.S. from the University of Missouri at Columbia. He is admitted to practice in Missouri and Kansas, as well as in the U.S. District Courts of the Western District of Missouri and the District of Kansas.

Acknowledgment: *I would like to thank Joshua M. Ellwanger, an associate at Husch Blackwell Sanders LLP, for his invaluable assistance in preparing for, participating in, and sharing the work of trial. This chapter and our successes in court could not have occurred without his—and our entire trial team's—help and support.*

I would also like to acknowledge the other law partners in our White-Collar Practice Group—Max Carr-Howard, Stephen L. Hill Jr., and Patrick A. McInerney—for their teamwork, cooperation, and collaboration, inside and outside the practice of law.

An Overview of Mortgage and Finance Fraud for Trustees

Neil C. Gordon

Partner

Arnall Golden Gregory LLP

ASPATORE

Introduction

My practice is focused on bankruptcy law, which involves virtually every legal discipline: real estate law, intellectual property, health care, and crimes involving civil or criminal fraud. I have been a federal bankruptcy trustee for seventeen years and have handled almost 20,000 individual and business cases. As a trustee, I have developed expertise in bankruptcy crimes, financial crimes, and mortgage fraud. My referrals have resulted in prosecutions in all such areas, including mortgage fraud and Ponzi schemes.

The Scourge of Ponzi Schemes

The U.S. attorney's office has given high priority to investigating, indicting, and prosecuting Ponzi schemers. Madoff and other large-scale frauds put the issue in front of the public, but those scams have been with us for a long time. The latest round was triggered by a huge drop in asset values; so many people lost value in their stocks and investments that they turned to these individuals or firms with whom they had invested and asked for some or all of their money back. When the Ponzi schemers could not make the returns and no new investors were coming in, the house of cards collapsed.

Many of these cases end up in the bankruptcy courts, most in the $10 million to $20 million range. That seems small when you consider the Madoff case, but it is just as meaningful to the people who are losing their investments. In the smaller schemes, there are fewer investors. In one of the cases I am handling, the largest investor put $4 million into the scheme. However, if someone invests $500,000 in one of these schemes and that is his life savings, all of the retirement money he had set aside, or his kids' college education funds, it is everything to him. To a trustee, it is not important whether the investor has invested $500,000 or $500 million. Investors were defrauded.

Psychology of Ponzi Perpetrators

The one thing I have noticed about people who perpetuate Ponzi schemes is they seem to have a sociopathic personality. They are devoid of remorse and will actually continue the scheme (or another) until they are put behind bars. They never stop the behavior. I always argue that these cases should be given the highest level of priority by the U.S. attorney's office because they continue to scheme and create new victims, even when the original scheme is stopped, until they are prosecuted.

The Economic Crisis and Mortgage Fraud

There is a clear connection between the lack of due diligence in the mortgage industry and the financial crisis. It was clear to me for many years that there was no due diligence. I receive, under penalty of perjury, the debtor's statement of financial affairs (SOFA) and schedules. The SOFA is a detailed personal financial statement, and I sought the loan packages for the purchase or refinancing. What I found, typically, was that information differed radically between the loan application and the SOFA. For example, someone making $20,000 a year bought seven properties in a three-month period and every loan application had him employed at a different company with a six-figure income. Nobody checked the information, and nobody thought to ask for tax returns, which would have refuted the entire deal.

The sub-prime lenders knew these kinds of loans were going to fail at a rate far higher than typical mortgages. The sub-primes were bundled and sold to investors all over the world in securities so that the risk was spread worldwide. It was believed that even if you had a certain percentage of fraud or mistakes being made, the risk was spread worldwide, so no one institution or investment syndicate would be materially affected. However, such a high percentage of these sub-prime loans were failing that the risk could not be sufficiently dissipated.

The fact that Fannie Mae and Freddie Mac were given authority by Congress to compete in the sub-prime mortgage market is disturbing at best. So, instead of being conservative and taking less risk, they went in the other direction. They were actually competing, and it seemed nobody was getting hurt, and everyone was getting rich. Mortgage brokers were putting people into products they could not afford, telling them not to worry about rising adjustable rates because they could just refinance when the mortgage reset at a higher rate because the property would have appreciated.

When the bubble burst, it dragged down everything worldwide. To my knowledge, only four countries' banks were relatively unaffected by the crisis: Australia, Canada, Norway, and Israel. Canadian banks unloaded all their toxic mortgage assets before the meltdown, and the others were not invested in them. The Canadian system had roughly the same level of home ownership as we do in this country, but they did not have all of our problems. A home buyer has to make a substantial down payment to buy a home in Canada; it can be as high as 20 percent. In the United States, we started charging 0 percent and made it easy to walk away from a deal. Buyers had no skin in the game—and that raises another troubling question: If you have to lie on your application to qualify for a mortgage, could that be a signal that you probably cannot afford the home?

Inside Bad Mortgage Management

When a buyer puts 0 percent down and is rolling the closing costs into the loan, the buyer can walk into a closing and pay nothing. The buyer walks out with a home. If that same person were to rent an apartment or a house, the landlord would charge a security deposit and first and last month's rent. If the rent is $800 a month, the individual will pay $1,600 plus a security deposit. In the end, the buyer could be paying upfront $2,500 to rent, but can own for zero. For many people, that made a lot of sense even if they could not make the mortgage payments. It did not cost them anything, and they could walk away if it did not work out. It was a stupid system, and many people said so from the start.

It is horrifying that Fannie Mae and Freddie Mac were competing for those kinds of mortgage loans. There is plenty of blame to go around. The lenders did no due diligence and did not care. They originated the loan and sold it almost immediately, so they were making their money up front. There was no real investment on the part of buyers. Their credit was damaged, but most of the people in the subprime market had bad credit anyway, or they would not have been subprime borrowers.

The Role of the Bankruptcy Trustee

The role of a trustee who sees or believes that a crime has been committed is to get more information. A bankruptcy trustee is looking for assets to distribute to creditors, whether they are investors or second mortgage holders on a property that was not worth half the amount of the first mortgage. Through mortgage fraud, the second mortgage holder loaned money and became completely unsecured. They are just another creditor, as would be the case with a credit card debt, so in a bankruptcy case the trustee is trying to get money to these creditors. At the same time, the trustee is performing a statutory duty to refer to the appropriate authority evidence of criminal misconduct: 18 U.S.C. § 3057(a) (2010). The code section states that a judge or private trustee "having reasonable grounds for believing that any violation .... of this title or other laws of the United States relating to insolvent debtors, receiverships, or reorganization plans has been committed shall report to the appropriate United States attorney all the facts and circumstances of the case, the names of the witnesses and the offense or offenses believed to have been committed."

Assistance during Criminal Investigations

Another section, 28 U.S.C. § 586(a)(3)(F), requires the United States trustee to notify "the appropriate United States attorney of matters which relate to the occurrence of any action which may constitute a crime under the laws of the United States, and, on the request of the United States attorney, assisting the United States attorney in carrying out prosecutions based on such action." That particular code section encompasses any crime, not just a bankruptcy crime, and imposes a duty to assist, as well as to report evidence of crimes. Therefore, trustees develop as much information as they can on crimes they believe have been committed.

Types of Mortgage Fraud

Mortgage Fraud by Individuals in Bankruptcy

When an individual who participates in mortgage fraud is already in bankruptcy, it opens up more problems. The trustee can get that money back because those sales are in violation of bankruptcy law and unwind them. While there is a good-faith exception, if you are involved in bankruptcy and mortgage fraud, there is no good faith. Trustees can unwind them and distribute the money back to creditors.

Short Sale Mortgage Fraud

Short sale mortgage fraud is not well understood. Instead of inflating the value, the perpetrator deflates and convinces the lender to release its mortgage for much less than the payoff of that mortgage and far less than the property is actually worth and then "flipped" to a new buyer for the true fair market value. This has become more common since the housing bubble burst.

For example, a property was appraised by a lender who had no stake in the transaction for $270,000; the buyer was forging the seller's name onto the short sale application, but it was actually the buyer running the scheme. They went through a short sale service, which told them what to put in letters to the mortgage company about gunfire at night and what a horrible area the home was in. The lender performed no due diligence, as many did not during the subprime era.

The short sale service agency got a $6,000 fee; the buyer got a property he put under contract the next day for $75,000 more than he paid for it; and yet, here is the lender discounting it as a short sale. The property was flipped, and the second closing took place forty days after the buyer bought it; he netted a $75,000 gain. Then he bragged about it on the Internet, and the trustee printed the evidence and used it to sue him and the other parties to recover sums to distribute to the legitimate creditors.

Rescue Fraud

Another major type of mortgage fraud is rescue fraud. An individual is about to get foreclosed and, even though the property is worth much more, he has not refinanced. He accepts the fraudulent help and pays money for the service.

Unfortunately, the fraudulent entity does not make mortgage payments and just keeps the money or sells the property, and the closing attorney is given written instructions to issue multiple checks: the seller usually keeps the small check and endorses the big check(s) to the rescue fraud perpetrator who brought in the phony buyer and helped commit the mortgage fraud.

Rent-skimming Fraud

Another scam is the commercial real estate guru who offers to handle the purchase and management of rental properties while "helping" the investor build a real estate empire. The fraudulent individual buys properties on behalf of the commercial investor, promises to manage all aspects of the operation—including the mortgage payments—and fills the properties with tenants. They collect the rents and don't make any mortgage payments. They will skim all the rents until the properties are foreclosed, but neither the owner nor the tenant will know in advance about the foreclosure. This rent-skimming form of mortgage fraud is not flipping; the perpetrators are simply skimming the rents for as long as they can while ownership is under a third party's name and affecting only that other individual's credit.

Multiple Offenders

Trustees will often make referrals against the same individual for mortgage fraud, bankruptcy fraud, and tax fraud. It is rare to have one without the others in bankruptcy court. For example, as trustee in one case, I had an individual's tax returns going back a few years. I ran a title search on the grantor/grantee deed index in my state and noticed that the individual (who happened to be a certified residential appraiser) had numerous transfers and sales of property for large gains. When I looked at her SOFA—which is filed under penalty of perjury in a bankruptcy case—I saw only one of seven transactions disclosed. Upon examination of the tax returns, I discovered the gains from the other six transactions had not been disclosed. Because they were not disclosed in the bankruptcy case, the omission constituted a bankruptcy crime. Failure to report the gains in the tax returns is tax fraud. The purchase-and-flip scheme was mortgage fraud. Only one or two mortgage payments would get made by the new owner. The lender would foreclose and take back a property worth far less than the loan, even though the appraisals were just obtained. This same fraud was committed for numerous properties.

Involvement of Professionals as Co-Conspirators

Many times, the accused individual will state, "I didn't keep all the money. I shared it with my co-conspirators." The trustee and the U.S. attorney collect the names and find that it is the broker, the lender, the buyer, the appraiser—basically, all the people in the mortgage process. It always saddens me when I see lawyers or law firms involved in these rings, but we have had a number of real estate closing attorneys in Georgia disbarred after pleading guilty to involvement in mortgage fraud. As a trustee, I have had a hand in this. You have to clean up your own community if colleagues are engaging in criminal activity, especially when they are preying on the public.

For example, a law firm was doing so many things wrong that they could not even explain why they were doing certain things. We subpoenaed all of the closing documents involving two individuals engaged in the alleged mortgage fraud; it was astonishing what was going on and how much money was flowing through. The buyers were completely fictitious individuals who had nothing to do with the transactions in closing after closing. When I pointed that fact out to the lead attorney, who was practicing with two of her sisters, she acted genuinely distressed to learn it was taking place and had no idea. I showed her documents, including lien releases (that we obtained from her office by subpoena) that had been forged by one of her sisters, who also admitted to the crime during deposition, even misspelling the name being forged. The method of mortgage fraud was a hard one to detect, called phantom liens.

Phantom Liens

This is a very effective type of mortgage fraud. The home improvement lien was listed as a second mortgage on the closing statement and would be paid off at closing. But no work was ever done, and there was no real lien because the whole thing was invented. The people involved in the conspiracy collected the money. In one case, $250,000 went to a phantom lien company, which was just a name on paper. The invoices attached had the name at the top, but if you read the body, you'd have seen it listed another company's name. The conspirators removed the real company's name from an unrelated project and put the fraudulent name on the invoice. They listed a broker who would receive a commission at closing, but examination of the purchase and sale agreement revealed that there was no realtor involvement. In that particular case, an FBI agent ended up posing as a party to a closing. He was wearing a wire, and we learned that the same lawyers who showed so much concern and regret when I pointed out their mistakes and fraud were still up to their same old tricks several months later when the sting operation occurred. As a result, the law practice was shut down, and its errors and omissions (E&O) insurance was rescinded by its carrier because it was also defrauded. Interestingly, much of the fraud occurred after I had written a letter questioning the law firm's practices.

Straw Buyers

If you look at HUD settlement closing statements and the listing of mortgages, you can immediately discern when one is fraudulent. A debtor who bought many properties as a straw buyer realizes at some point that he has been duped. He has been told that he was going to "earn" more money.

Most people who come through bankruptcy are not willing to admit that they have been a straw buyer because that would make them a participant in mortgage fraud. I can recognize it when I see they have been involved in flips and quick sales. They may not want to admit it, but asking the right questions will reveal the facts. When I tell them that most of the straw buyers involved in that industry are paid around $10,000 per property, many debtors will say, "I only got $4,000." We find out who was involved and turn the names over to the U.S. attorney

Common Types of Financial and Credit Fraud

Bustouts

Credit Card Bustouts

What we do on the front end of a bankruptcy case is investigate all the financial affairs; we call it a fishing expedition. For example, an individual from Nigeria had several hundred thousand dollars of credit card debt. He filed bankruptcy and was looking to discharge the debt. When I asked for an explanation of what the debt was used for and why he was not showing any property, he was reluctant and evasive. I advised him that the case could not go forward and he could not get a discharge without a full explanation. When he continued to refuse, I subpoenaed his credit card records. He eventually started to open up and explain. This individual was going to auto auctions, buying cars on his credit cards, and then shipping the cars to his uncle in Nigeria. The uncle never paid for any of the cars, and this individual filed bankruptcy to discharge the debts that resulted from financing the purchase of cars that were not even in this country any longer. This is a credit card bustout. The same kind of fraud occurs with appliances.

Many individuals will try to say they lost the money gambling, but when we ask them for records, they say they do not have them. In one case, the person produced one month of statements on one credit card, and I saw about $12,000 in jewelry had been purchased a month before the bankruptcy. The individual did not report it, but when pressed, said that he gave it to his mother. Yet he had not listed any gifts or gambling losses, either. I referred that to the U.S. attorney for credit card fraud, and the individual was convicted of both bankruptcy and credit card fraud.

Inventory Bustout

An inventory bustout occurs when a buyer takes over a company and starts buying small amounts on credit from the same vendors. As the company continues to establish good credit, the company suddenly orders far more inventory than usual, then sells it, pockets the money, and puts the company into bankruptcy. There is no money or assets for the trustee to use, and the perpetrator disappears. A variation is to keep the large inventory and file bankruptcy. The secured lender gets more collateral, so there is no call on the company owner's personal guarantee.

Bank Loan Fraud

A few years ago, a bank client sent me a loan it wanted handled in a bankruptcy case. The loan was relatively small, around $40,000. We could not find any of the assets that were listed on the loan application for this individual and obtained a judgment in the bankruptcy court that the debt had to be paid, notwithstanding the bankruptcy case. 11 U.S.C. § 523. About six months later, the same bank sent us another loan that looked similar to the earlier one. Both involved Korean individuals, and the loan applications were filled out by someone with the same handwriting. We called this to the attention of the bank, and an audit of the loan portfolio was conducted. At different levels of the bank, loan officers had different loan limits under their purview. These loans were within those limits. Three different bank clients of mine were being defrauded by Korean "loan brokers."

The criminals were loan brokers advertising in the Korean language newspapers offering business loans with 15 percent to 30 percent upfront as the fees. If the individual wanted to borrow $500,000, a 30 percent fee would be $150,000. The loan brokers were filling out all the applications and creating phony businesses, then seeking operating loans and equipment purchase loans. There was no equipment or operations. When the bank filed their financing statements, which is what a bank files in the public records to show they have a security interest, the collateral did not exist. Therefore, the bank was an unsecured creditor. I discovered this not as a bankruptcy trustee, but as a bankruptcy lawyer for a bank client. We found out that there were two different bank fraud rings operating in the Korean community with more than thirty individuals involved. Many fled the country; the ones who were still here got indicted and convicted, but not before the banks lost many millions of dollars.

The banks did not realize the fraud was being committed because their loans were current. If an individual borrows $500,000 and pays the loan broker $150,000, the borrower still has $350,000 in net proceeds. If the loan payment is $5,000 monthly, the payment is coming from the borrowed money. The bank was being repaid out of the same money it had loaned. The banks did not realize they had a problem. When I called it to their attention, they conducted audits, and their security staffs discovered the problem. By teaming up with the FBI, they were able to find the offenders and have them prosecuted.

Bankruptcy Rules and Criminal Prosecution

Debts that Can Be Discharged under Fraud

When fraud occurs in bankruptcy, different rules come into effect. Code section 11 U.S.C. § 523 defines which kind of debts cannot be discharged in bankruptcy if someone files a complaint. If an entity is defrauded, it can object to someone discharging that debt and prevent him or her from walking away from it.

For one of my most recent Ponzi schemers, we objected successfully to his total discharge under 11 U.S.C. § 727; however, he is still defrauding people because he has not yet been indicted. A local news channel did a segment on him that was interesting and well done, showing the two Mercedes, the Freightliner, and Rolexes that he acquired with the investors' money. He never invested a single penny, but was living off the money his clients turned over to him to invest. Fabricated financial statements were sent to the investors. That is typical for a Ponzi schemer.

Fraudulent Transfers

A person transferring property through fraud in a bankruptcy case is violating the law. United States Code Sections 544 and 548 address fraudulent transfers, and Section 550 deals with the recovery of the fraudulent transfers.

In a Ponzi scheme, the entire enterprise is a fraud, so these provisions are implicated automatically. People view themselves as victims even if they have gotten all their original investment and some profit. If the promised return is less than what they were originally promised, they feel defrauded. The trustees will sue them, and they will have to turn over that profit. This is an evolving area of the law: one view is that even the investors who lost money have to turn over what they received in the way of repayments. In other words, they did not make a profit. Suppose an individual invested $1 million and should have had a $1.5 million return on the investment, but they had drawn out $300,000. One view is that if that $300,000 was paid within four years of the bankruptcy after they knew or should have known about the existence of the fraud, then that can be recovered. The trustee distributes the funds on a pro rata basis to everyone. Investors get upset if they have to pay back such "dividends."

Bleedouts

Bleedouts can be subtle. The assets are transferred to a similarly named company, and the shell of the old company with the liabilities goes into bankruptcy. The trustee has nothing with which to work because there is nothing there. The key is for the trustee to find that the receivables were collected from the old company and put into the new company. Bleedouts can be pursued as standard fraudulent transfers, but an important difference is that they are criminal bankruptcy fraud schemes. The fraud does not involve finance companies; it is being committed against the creditors of the old company.

SIPA Trustees and SEC Receivers

In the Madoff situation, there are other variables because a Securities Investment Protection Act (SIPA) trustee is in place and has different rules. A SIPA trustee is not just a normal bankruptcy trustee and follows a different set of laws. Many of these cases end up in bankruptcy, although many do not. Others finish with a Securities and Exchange Commission (SEC) receivership action. The SEC has gotten a great deal of bad press because they never discovered Madoff, even though people had been complaining. But Ponzi schemers are quite clever. If the SEC gets a receiver appointed, often it just liquidates and pursues assets and lawsuits outside of bankruptcy. Sometimes the receiver will file a bankruptcy because it does not believe there is any money to pay the cost of the receivership and does not know how it will pay its professionals. The receiver might then become the bankruptcy trustee.

The trustee can pull in monies from creditors that were repaid as preference and fraudulent transfers. 11 U.S.C. §§ 544, 547, 548, 550. This will provide money from which to operate and pursue bigger causes of actions around the world. Many SEC receiverships end up in bankruptcy because the bankruptcy is filed by the Ponzi schemer to impede the receiver. Then the debtor will be taken over by a bankruptcy trustee.

With a Ponzi scheme, the receiver or trustee must move quickly because the schemer will conceal its assets. In one of my Ponzi scheme cases soon after I was appointed as Chapter 11 trustee, we got orders to seize houses, cars, and boats. However, the schemer still concealed assets and failed to comply with order after order. We required him to show cause why he should not be held in contempt because he was still concealing assets and talking about being a pauper living out of his car. He did not know where his expensive boat was or his Rolexes or his passport. (A passport should be surrendered to the receiver or trustee.) We also asked for his computers, laptops, passwords, cell phones, and BlackBerrys.

Collecting Evidence from Electronic Devices

When asked on the witness stand whether he had his cell phone and Palm Treo with him, the schemer said no. When asked whether he had them when he tried to enter the federal courthouse, he said yes. Security had taken and was holding them, and I got the judge to order the U.S. Marshal to retrieve them. We learned that earlier the same day he was trying to renew his season tickets for four floor seats to the Atlanta Hawks games— some pauper.

Handheld devices and laptops help a trustee or court track information because one of the hallmarks of Ponzi schemers is they keep poor records of where everything is. That is intentional, so if they had records, they would destroy them before officials could get their hands on them. Hard drives and other handheld devices will reveal a substantial amount of information. The individual in this example was given one hour to refresh his recollection or he would be incarcerated. In that hour, his passports and Rolexes showed up; he remembered where his boat was; and other assets suddenly appeared because he did not want to go to jail.

You have to move fast with fraudulent debtors because they can hide the assets. When they file the Chapter 11, they think they are in control and can hold onto the assets. Once the trustee or an SEC receiver appears, it is a race to see if you can get to the assets before they can be concealed. One schemer tried to persuade me that if he continued his scheme, he could raise enough to pay off his investors. While that was likely true, he would be defrauding a new set of investors.

Advice for Trustees

The economy is hard hit; many people are out of work and struggling with debt; and bankruptcy filings are increasing; but there are always new scammers preying on the most financially disadvantaged—for example, offering to settle debts for a fee. I believe only one in ten of those companies is legitimate. People are turning over the few dollars they have left to these new scam artists who promise to solve problems, such as settling their debts or modifying their mortgages. Instead, they just collect the money, do nothing, and leave the victims helpless.

Unfortunately, bankruptcy lawyers who represent the consumer never allocate any time to understanding whether fraud has been committed. In nearly 20,000 cases, I have never been told by a consumer attorney that the client was a victim of mortgage fraud. The attorney is there to try to get his or her client a discharge of debt. In fact, if an attorney even hints that there was an irregularity, it could get the client in trouble because he or she may have been the straw buyer, and his or her credit was used to buy the properties. A straw buyer is also a participant in the mortgage fraud, but is not regularly prosecuted because he or she is not the ring leader and is a victim, too. However, the individual is still a co-conspirator, which is a fact that the attorney does not want the trustee or U.S. attorney to know.

Trustees must become familiar with the telltale signs of fraud. For example, in a Chapter 7 matter, the U.S. attorney will not see the case, nor will the judge. The trustee may be the only person examining the case. As the gatekeeper, if the trustee does not make the determination that a crime has been committed, it is likely to go undetected.

Learning the Signs of Fraud

The trustee should become familiar with the tell tale signs of mortgage fraud: flipping of property usually indicates mortgage fraud, where properties are being sold in relatively short order with ever higher sale prices. If a property is sold in a bankruptcy case without court authority, but the sale proceeds do not hit the debtor's bank account, there is a good chance that it is mortgage fraud. When sale proceeds go to the buyer as a kickback, they violate the Real Estate Settlement Procedures Act (RESPA). Massive credit card debt with no property is another clue; the trustee should insist on a legitimate answer about how the credit was used, review the credit card statements, and, if the debtor cannot provide a sufficient answer, make a criminal referral. If a company in bankruptcy has no accounts receivable or bank balance, a bleedout may be in process.

Key Takeaways

- Mortgage loans, bank business loans, or credit card activity undertaken without due diligence is an open door to mortgage or financial fraud.

- Get familiar with the telltale signs: property flipping in relatively short order with either very high or very low sale prices is a sign of mortgage fraud.

- Sale proceeds much greater than the bank deposit by the seller is a sign of mortgage fraud.

- The trustee must move expeditiously when dealing with potential fraud. Debtors will try to hide assets, and passports should be requested immediately.

- Any devices that provide access to information must be confiscated by the trustee, including computers, laptop computers, all access codes and passwords, mobile phones, PDAs, and smart phones.

- The trustee is in the best position to make a criminal referral. If the trustee does not do so during the bankruptcy proceeding, the crime will likely go undetected.

Neil C. Gordon is a partner in the bankruptcy and reorganization department of the Atlanta law firm, Arnall Golden Gregory LLP. After graduating from the University of Georgia's Lumpkin School of Law in 1979, he served for two years as a law clerk in Atlanta for United States District Court Judge Robert L. Vining Jr. For the following twenty-eight years, he has been in private practice, the last twenty-five years being exclusively in the areas of bankruptcy, business reorganization, and creditors' rights.

Mr. Gordon chaired the Bankruptcy Law Section of the Atlanta Bar Association from 1992 to 1993 and has been a panel trustee since 1994. He has administered approximately 19,000 Chapter 7 and Chapter 11 cases. He was first elected to the board of the National Association of Bankruptcy Trustees in 2000 and currently serves as its vice president.

Mr. Gordon is on the editorial board of the Journal of the National Association of Bankruptcy Trustees *and co-authors the "Recent Cases" article for each quarterly issue. He is the author of "The Art of the Carve-Out," which appears in the* Journal's *spring 2009 issue. Mr. Gordon is also on the editorial board of the* ABI Journal, *and his article, "Federal Crimes: The Trustee's Role," appears in the December 2009/January 2010 issue.*

Mr. Gordon is the education director of the ABI's Legislation Committee. He lectures frequently at regional and national seminars throughout the country. He has served on the faculty of the National Bankruptcy Training Institute and is a Fellow of the American College of Bankruptcy.

Client Strategies for Counteracting Mortgage Fraud

Robert R. Maddox

Partner

Bradley Arant Boult Cummings LLP

ASPATORE

Introduction

Our practice is focused on representing financial institutions, such as banks, mortgages companies, and related businesses. We specialize in both litigation and regulatory compliance. On the mortgage related litigation, it runs the gamut from advertising of the origination of the loan to the closing; we are also involved in warehouse lending, transfer selling, securitization, servicing the mortgage loan, and commercial disputes between mortgage companies.

Our clients range from large depository institutions to small vendor support companies. We are fortunate that our clients have asked us to represent them across the United States, which has led us from handling fair lending complaints in Oakland, California to working with the New York State Banking Department to trials in the Southern District of Florida and to assisting on QWR responses in Waterloo, Iowa.

Recent Fraud Trends

The biggest trends right now in mortgage fraud are a direct result of the current economic environment. So many people are currently facing foreclosures and defaults. The foreclosure tsunami wiped across America and cut across socio-economic demographics. It is not a problem only in inner cities or rural areas, but in affluent communities as well. A cross section of America is yelling loudly about the default and foreclosure crisis, while there are also people preying on the most downtrodden people in America. Short sale frauds, foreclosure fraud schemes, and loan modification frauds are currently the most common problems.

As the mortgage industry turned from focusing on origination to servicing—as the credit crisis has caused a flight to security and conventional loans—prior origination channels where we were focused on origination fraud have correspondingly decreased—flipping, credit packing, equity skimming, identity theft, straw buyers, and "real estate" investor schemes. Now we are seeing fraud that is more specific to handling the default crisis. Foreclosures obviously occurred during the boom of this cycle and there was minimal fraud in the real estate owned (REO) market; however, during the boom, as property values were increasing, short sales and loan modifications were possible loss mitigation possibilities but they were seldom seen.

Shakeout in the Real Estate Industry

Over the past thirty months, white collar enforcement groups at the federal and state levels have taken a great deal of interest in commercial and residential mortgage fraud. They are much more likely to pursue the case, which has been a benefit to the industry as a whole. Given the current economic downturn, there is much more general interest and the pointing of fingers at the real estate industry for some of the blame that led to the global economic recession. The law enforcement arms of the federal and state governments pursuing those interests consider this a win-win situation.

I think this increased focus is a benefit for the industry because, when its members testify, they reveal the bad apples that took advantage of the system during the boom times. These are the true corporate citizens of America: they are trying to eradicate fraud from their own industry. The perpetrators must pay—in the civil and criminal sense—for the harm they caused. Mortgage fraud can easily wreck someone's life if they become immersed in a loan modification or foreclosure group scam that pushes them into losing their home. An effective, efficient member of society becomes homeless, or without a home in which they have an interest, and it can have a devastating effect on an individual's life. I am confident that the financial institutions want people to succeed in home ownership by making their payments. When you see these people go down for the fraud that they have committed, it enables the industry to police itself. I hope it provides the American public with a bit of distaste for what the individuals have done, but that it also underscores the fact that the industry is trying to correct itself.

The Short Sale Scam

Not long ago, prior to 2009, the mortgage companies would simply move the property through foreclosure and then market it themselves. Given the amount of inventory and REO properties on the market, every property listed that went through foreclosure had an impact on the market value of that property. If it is a foreclosed property, it is fair to say to a prospective purchaser that, "the bank owns this property and it is costing them money every day that they are holding it." The bank has to pay taxes, insurance, and a realtor to market it, so the buyer will low-ball an offer. Because so much inventory is out there, the mortgage companies and investors are selling property at a steeply discounted rate. In this short sale phenomenon, borrowers are trying to get out from under the liability so that they will not have a foreclosure on their credit report.

In a typical short sale, a borrower who is unable to make his payment has worked with the mortgage servicer to try to sell the property. Both sides of the equation—borrower and mortgager/servicer—will lose money but there is a cost benefit analysis: if they try to sell the property out on the open market it benefits the borrower so they will not move through foreclosure. It benefits the servicer and the investor because they can liquidate assets rather than foreclose, take it through REO, pay taxes and insurance, and ultimately market it anyway.

Realtors receive compensation from selling properties, so they are extremely aggressive in trying to short sale these homes. Consider an example where the borrower and the mortgage company agree to sell a house for $250,000. The realtor who is working on that short sale has knowledge that other people may be interested down the line, so he or she will set up back-to-back transactions. After the house sells for $250,000, the realtor may turn right around and sell that property again in the afternoon for a $100,000 profit. The same situation can occur with closing agents or closing attorneys. They get paid to close the loan, so if they sell the same piece of property twice in a day they are getting paid twice. This phenomenon has increased in the last year and is growing quite rapidly.

In order to counteract these scams, we have either stopped the short sale, or have gone back and rescinded it. Then we go after the realtor, appraiser, closing attorney, the short sale purchaser, and the person they ultimately sold it to again. The goal is to unwind the transaction and return the property to REO status, and then remarket it. On limited occasions in the past, we sold the property to the same individual or entity who was the subsequent purchaser after we determined they were an innocent party to the original transaction.

Foreclosure and Loan Modification Fraud Schemes

In a distressed borrowers' context, the borrower may be in default because of job loss, divorce, or death in the family—we usually just label this as a "life-altering" situation that the borrower had no control over. This life altering event has prevented the borrower(s) from making their mortgage payment—thus, the borrower(s) are in default.

We believe you must step in the shoes of the borrower(s) to understand why they may fall prey to a scam artist. You need to think about the borrower from a psychological standpoint. The borrower(s) are in default on the mortgage, and likely also on unsecured obligations such as credit cards. Creditors are calling constantly, voicemails left on their answering machines, multiple letters, and correspondence from their creditors or debt collectors are becoming routine. They are in a desperate situation with no clear path to saving their home and credit.

One day, the borrower picks up the phone and someone is telling them their name and who is holding their mortgage loan. To the average person, a caller who has detailed information about their mortgage is naturally reputable.[1] But what the borrower may not realize is that information about their loan is public information. This situation opens the door for mortgage fraud. The caller offers to help them with a loan, but what they are really offering is a foreclosure or loan modification scheme. They get their first hook into the borrower by providing them with this information, and they claim to work with "all the big companies," such as Wells Fargo, Bank of America, and so on. An offer of loan modification follows—which can be either a loan modification or a stop on a foreclosure. Instead of the borrower trying to make some form of payment to the mortgage company, the borrower pays the fraud company anywhere from $500 to $5,000 and expects help. In many cases, the defrauders do nothing except take the up front fee. Sometimes the scammers will try to contact the mortgage servicer

---

[1] The way we foreclose on homes in America depends on the state. In judicial states, we file a lawsuit against the borrower and provide the name of the borrower, the place of residence, the property address, and sometimes the defaulting company. The case will be ABC Bank v. John Smith, and the creditor will state how much money is owed because they are trying to foreclose. In non-judicial states in which we have power of sale, we will advertise a public auction so the entire matter is a transparent transaction and, hopefully, the property can go to its highest price.

in order to cover themselves in the event the fraud is discovered—as they are careful not to guarantee results.

In many instances, the scammers will tell the borrower not to make contact with the mortgage servicer. The scammer does not want the borrower to hear conflicting information. In fact, it will tell the borrower that he or she needs to authorize them to speak on their behalf. The borrower(s) execute a document allowing the scammers to be an "authorized third party" to their account. (This is exactly what a legitimate credit counselor would do, except they usually would only make contact with the servicer while the borrower(s) are also on the telephone call.) Communications between the borrower and the mortgage company will cease, and the borrower will fall months behind until finally they receive a foreclosure notice and their house is about to be sold. Only then does the borrower call the mortgage company, which states that it has been talking to the third party that the borrower authorized, and that the loss mitigation process has stalled. The result is a borrower who is much further behind, a servicer that has to deal with a property on the cusp of foreclosure, an investor that is going to lose money, and a scammer who has preyed on the most financially vulnerable but will make off with the up front fee and maybe even the title to the property in the short term.

Aggressive Enforcement by Attorneys General

Since the spring of 2008, state attorneys general have been pursuing lawsuits involving foreclosure and loan modification scams. Nearly every state attorney general's Web site lists these scams because they want it known that they are pursuing them. These lawsuits are clearly important to the state attorney generals, as it shows they are attempting to protect their state citizens from falling prey to the scams as outlined above. California and Nevada have been particularly aggressive in this, while New York, Minnesota, Ohio, North Carolina, and Texas are taking active roles and are fertile ground for court cases. From strictly a media standpoint, the attorney general has a bully pulpit from which to work, and has the entire state government behind him or her. If an attorney general calls a press conference, people are always going to show up to report it. These lawsuits are much more newsworthy than when a mortgage servicer sues a loan modification or foreclosure scam company.

Loan Modification Frauds Involving Investment Properties

Origination of loans and documentation has become much more restricted lately due to the credit crisis and tougher underwriting standards. We are not seeing as much origination fraud, but people are submitting loan modification documents that are inaccurate or that misrepresent their resources and liabilities. For example, during the past few years, borrowers who bought multiple investment properties may now be behind in their payments. When they seek a loan modification, they fail to acknowledge the full extent of their liability from ownership of multiple properties—they only list the liability of the particular property where they are seeking the loan modification. Many people bought second homes in the states of California, Arizona, and Florida (the so-called "sand states"); yet claim that their residence is in Kansas. If you did a title search in Kansas, you would not discover that they had investment properties elsewhere. Even if you found their home, the property may likely be serviced by another mortgage company. A loan modification may provide some relief, but it will ultimately fail again because of outstanding liabilities and the borrower has committed fraud by misrepresenting their true outstanding liabilities. Another twist on this same theme, is that the borrower when confronted with the misrepresentation in failing to list all their investment properties will now claim that they did indeed have prior residence in another state and that the underlying property was originally investment but now they have moved and made the former investment property their permanent residence.

Buy and Bails

A related major trend in 2009 is what we termed "buy and bails." Borrowers who bought at the height of the market owed, for example, $500,000 on their house, and then received a notice that they were going to lose their job. This would make it difficult or impossible for them to afford the house. Down the street, there is a nearly identical house already in foreclosure that is on the market for $200,000. The borrower(s) then fabricate a rental agreement for their current $500,000 house and use false rental income to obtain the new home down the street for $200,000. They still have their job at the time they buy the second home. However, when they are laid off, they let the first home fall into foreclosure. The borrowers justify their actions as they were planning on a credit hit anyway, so they have effectively reduced their liability and the amount owed by buying a similar house. However, the borrowers may not view this as fraud, but they falsified their income and a rental agreement—and it is fraud!

Fraud in Bankruptcies

With the downturn in the economy, we are seeing more fraud that affects the servicer of the loan. In some cases, right before a borrower files their bankruptcy petition, they transfer the property. That action violates the "due on sale clause" of the mortgage. In other cases, as a delay tactic, one spouse files bankruptcy so only an undivided half interest in the property goes into the bankruptcy and the other assets stay out. Obtaining a fraudulent appraisal on the property in order to strip off a secured lien and trying to convert it from a secured lien to an unsecured lien is another common tactic. We have also seen a debtor receive bankruptcy court approval to sell a house and a property and then they set up a fraudulent sale to a straw buyer either to keep the house or to strip out the remaining equity.

Lawsuits filed by Borrowers only for the Purpose of Delay

We are also seeing a tsunami of pre-emptive lawsuits by delinquent borrowers who are just trying to delay—their allegations are baseless and made in bad faith. They will allege payment misapplication, escrow misapplication, servicing noncompliance, and even allegations of origination fraud that occurred years ago. At times, borrowers will even switch their mailing addresses around and claim to not have received proper notice as another form of delay.

In 2008 and 2009, a number of consumer attorneys stated in court documents that they represented distressed borrowers and were filing lawsuits on their behalf. After we defended some lawsuits, we actually found out that the borrowers didn't know they were being represented by the attorneys. To further complicate and already difficult situation, many attorneys are defending consumers for the first time in this area and they do not have expertise or much less even a basic understanding of real property.

State and Federal Regulations

In general, fraud is a state law claim, though some federal laws are clearly applicable depending on the allegations—TILA, RESPA, FCRA/FACTA, etc. If servicing or origination fraud occurs, there is usually wire fraud, RICO, and other federal statutes that deal with this area. Legislation is coming out of the states that attempts to regulate foreclosure scams or loan modification groups; those laws go hand-in-hand with many of the actions that the attorneys general are taking. Loan modification and foreclosure groups are becoming a cottage industry, and the legislation appears to be intended to regulate them to ensure that they are not defrauding the public. There has been a push at the federal level for new compliance matters, some of which will take effect but do not necessarily have a greater impact. States are now focusing on the loan modification and foreclosure groups and requirements necessary for them to be good corporate citizens in each individual state. On the whole, there has not been a great deal of evolution in the fraud legislation arena. By trying to regulate small-industry debt modification, the intent is to get rid of the bad actors. New requirements include capital reserves, licensure, and proof of benefit to the borrower.

Strategies for Dealing with Mortgage Fraud Cases

It the fraud is current, the attorney should move expeditiously and file a temporary restraining order (TRO) to stop whatever the client perceives as fraudulent activity. The attorney must secure assets for potential recovery, especially if the defrauders are bad actors. The steps in the strategy include:

1. If the fraud is underway, try to stop it immediately with a TRO and then engage in expedited discovery.
2. Request bank documents, checking accounts, wire transfers, and begin to track the money as it moved through the fraudulent process. For example, if money was deposited in Bank A and part of that money went to Bank B, we would then subpoena Bank B for those documents.
3. Assess where the damage lies and try to discern which money was moved around the country through wire transfers and other mechanisms.

4. Determine whether additional causes of action exist, and add additional parties as necessary. There is usually a number of settlement overtures to stop the action before it gets any bigger. At that point, the client has the opportunity to make a cost benefit analysis whether or not to proceed forward on a civil matter.

5. Try to settle the matter if the fraud has been eradicated from the system. Otherwise, move on and take depositions in the case. Those are fun, in a sad way, because people may just plead the Fifth Amendment the entire time or their memory will become so absent they cannot answer their own name. You can wrap them up pretty tight at that point.

6. Before you reach the trial, determine if the fraud has been eradicated, if the recovery has been maximized, or if the client can be made whole by the settlement.

Involvement of Criminal Prosecutors

While we are putting our civil case together, we are assembling the same information for delivery to federal and state authorities, through the state attorney general, the district attorney, or the FBI. We can position the client as a good corporate citizen, explain the actions that occurred, and ask the authorities to investigate. At that point, it has converted to a criminal action; the civil suit may continue forward, but it usually limps along because you have brought in the authorities. You may hear about a grand jury, or get subpoenaed. Of course, the law enforcement authorities cannot tell you what they are doing or how they are doing it and it may be a matter of months or years before there is an indictment. That is, ultimately, the end of the attorney's involvement. There is a civil charge and a civil recovery. On the criminal side, depending on the caseload and the amount in controversy, the federal or state authorities may find it in their interest to pursue the case.

Best Practices for Prosecuting Mortgage Fraud

In mortgage fraud cases, you need to gather as much information as possible, through methods such as asset sheets, record title documents and background searches, and then use that data to reconstruct the puzzle that the fraudster originally built. It is like trying to construct a one hundred-piece puzzle and starting out with only twenty of the pieces and you are not sure what the final puzzle is supposed look like. You have to go back to their origination files, check bank documents, and interview any witnesses who were involved. Then it is a matter of trying to piece together what happened and presenting that argument to both the client and to the court. You have to connect all of the dots to demonstrate that there is a case of clear fraud. Unless you can connect those dots between the fraudulent act itself, misrepresentation, the benefit, and the bad actor, the proof will fall short.

Fraud cases are fun because you get to be a lawyer, an investigator and, when you serve a TRO on a company, a force for justice. However, there is a lot of work in big fraud cases because you have to ensure that there are no loose ends.

TROs

A unique aspect of our practice is that when we receive telephone calls about a fraud, we will prepare a temporary restraining order (TRO) complaint, and we will move for an *ex parte* TRO to stop whatever type of current mortgage fraud is involved. There is a flood of e-mails and information that help put together the best complaint and TRO that you can. If another entity is involved, such as the closing attorney or a title agent, we will move to shut down their operations. This creates some risk for our client: the entity or person may be committing fraud, but if you freeze their bank accounts, you run the risk of completely shutting down their organization. While the client's money is preserved in the accounts, the claim has shut down a small business. There may be risk for a counter claim with regard to disruption of business.

When you get into court, you then have to argue to the judge why such an extreme measure is necessary. You have to have your documents in place and may even have a witness or two, so it is like a small one-sided trial to get the TRO and have it served by process server. At times, we have taken a newly signed TRO and served it on the business directly. The situation moves very quickly and you never know what will happen when you are dealing with people who have stolen money or have misrepresented a mortgage documents. If they are willing to steal hundreds of thousands or millions of dollars, what kind of person are you about to meet on the other side of that door

We do TROs frequently, and while it is fun and exhilarating, you have to move quickly. On the flip side, if fraud is being committed and we are trying to collect money, we will gather as much documentation and information as possible and make an early cost benefit analysis as to whether there is potential for recovery. We have to balance the ultimate goal of stopping any type of liability to our client from the fraud and ensuring that there are assets to recover. Many times, a wrongdoer does not have the wherewithal to pay on a judgment or settlement agreement, so again a cost-benefit analysis is critical.

Resources Needed for a Successful Case

In a fraud case, we typically represent the servicer. Even if origination fraud occurred, once that loan is originated and sold, a servicer has to hold and deal with it. We will use origination documents as a primary source, and if forgery was committed we call an expert witness in handwriting. The title policy is an important document. When dealing with a fraud on the property or by the closing attorney, you have to go back to see if there is coverage underneath the title insurance. If there was fraud at the closing table, there is an insured closing protection letter that the title insurance company issues to the lender that, in most aspects, goes down the line with the assignees and assignors. It is possible to recover underneath but can be difficult. If you are looking at appraisal fraud, you would go back and look at the short form report to see how fair market value, sales price, and loan value were determined. The valuation method the appraiser used, such as the income approach or cost approach, is important, and if the mortgage broker is involved you would go back and look at their original documents. Communication with the borrower, relative to determine what was said and offered, can provide valuable insight into the status of a loan. If a loan came through the wholesale channel, you must go back and look at who originated the loan. If it was someone who bought the loan, then you can go back and see how it was underwritten and examine documents or contracts between the correspondent lender and the ultimate investor. At the same time, you are creating a case for the originator to potentially repurchase the fraudulent loan.

Length of the Process for Fraud Matters

If the case is a single file, it can be completed within a matter of months. In some cases, once you approach the company about the fraud, then they will try to work it out in a civil matter. However, if it is a complex case then it can go on for far longer. For example, I have been working on one case that has lasted for three years. We went in with a TRO and took over an entire practice of a closing agent, secured their files, did a detailed analysis, and worked through a civil settlement. Then the state Bar Association, the FBI, and U.S. Attorney came in and the criminal process moved forward. While dealing with all of the abovementioned parties, there is also the need to capture any type of malpractice insurance and determine whether the wrongdoing was actual fraud or only negligence. If it is fraud, there may not be any coverage, but if there is malpractice, there should be coverage. The tangential litigation with the insurance companies will occur simultaneously to the civil and criminal matters.

The Complex Aspects of Mortgage Fraud Cases

The most complex cases involve multiple entities. For example, in one case a broker, real estate agent, and closing attorney (who was also a title agent) were all involved in producing fraudulent mortgages. We filed a TRO, closed down the practice, secured all of the existing files, and shut down their bank accounts. From that point, the best strategy is to lean hard on whoever is available. If an attorney is involved, they also have to deal with repercussions from the state bar association. In my experience, the broker will try to throw blame on everyone else involved in the process. The complexity arises when a broker is able to pull in their insurance company to defend them. The insurance company defends them under the reservation of rights, asserting that it is negligence, not fraud. Those cases can go on for quite some time, but when you are dealing with fraud for profit, the key is to track the money.

We have developed an approach found to be successful in dealing with these cases. Once you get the first closing file, you begin subpoenaing to determine where the money went. Tracking the money enables you to find the exit point. Fraudsters who engage in mortgage fraud typically like to buy more property and they will use their ill-gotten gains as a down payment, or for a boat or a car. If they buy property, they will put a mortgage on it and we will claim an equitable interest in that property. Even if it runs through multiple banks and, ultimately, $200,000 comes out to purchase a piece of property, we will claim an interest in that property because our clients' money was used to purchase the property. We will secure other assets the same way. This process mirrors an IRS tax lien or a criminal forfeiture. The property is secured, sold, and the client gets the remaining proceeds. Tracking the money and assets takes time because you have to subpoena the bank and wait for them to give you the documents to review. If you do not have enough information, you have to return to the bank and request more documentation. Tracking money in this manner takes time, but its scope is fairly limited. However, if you can eradicate the fraud, achieve a successful recovery for your client, and remove a fraudulent person from the industry, the case is successful.

The Client's Role in the Fraud Case Process

The client has to make the decision—with the advice of counsel—about the next steps. Is everyone inside the fraud nexus together? Are there people who were tangentially involved that we do not want involved? Are there entities or companies whose relationship to the fraud needs to be clarified—and were they aware of the fraud? We can provide an estimated budget and cost benefit analysis relative to assets, whether or not they are encumbered, and the probability of a recovery. Unlike regular litigation, which is driven almost exclusively by the finances involved, with fraud cases, clients are more apt to move both with a cost benefit analysis and the principle of the matter. The client may not want to see the person come back into the industry in any role. This is healthy because it is doing the right thing to remove that person from the industry.

The client always has the final say, and we provide the advice, assessment, and strategy with which to get to the end goal. That goal may change from the beginning of the lawsuit to the end. Depending on the fraudulent party's reaction, we could have an agreement in principal within a week and a final agreement in place within three to four weeks.

Settlement versus Litigation

Whether to settle or litigate depends on the client and the nature of the fraud. A complex fraud entity executing provocative and pervasive fraud that may affect the company over the long term might warrant staying in the case and litigating. A single fraud file is more likely to go away on a cost benefit analysis and be settled.

Consider the mortgage industry and its basic setup: wholesale brokers have been maligned in the press because their goal is to close a transaction with no pecuniary or financial interest in whether the loan actually performs or whether the borrower is able to stay in the house. The wholesale broker's goal from a professional and financial standpoint is to originate the loan and sell it off immediately if it was a table funded loan, or to be able to sell it off within thirty to sixty days. They want to make as much money off the transaction as possible. If you move that investment along and it goes from a broker to a warehouse and, ultimately, to an investor; and that investor decides that there was something wrong in the origination of that file, it will push it back down to the servicer who is working directly with the borrower for repurchase. In turn, the servicer would go after the originator and potentially other parties involved in the origination of the loan, and then on up the inverted pyramid.

There are national or international companies at the very top of the pyramid, who, despite recent economic events, are much more capitalized than the broker who originated the single loan. They push it all the way down and the broker may not have the capital to repurchase. A broker who commits fraud and makes from $2,000 to $20,000 off a large mortgage origination and created a $1 million loan may not have the ability to repurchase the loan if it violated the selling requirements. That is one of the big problems facing the industry. Repurchase demands being pushed back down are restraining the servicers, and they are looking at the corresponding lender or wholesaler that does not have the financial resources to repurchase. Essentially, the system has produced an invalid or defaulting loan for $1 million with no way to repurchase. In a fraud case, look at the assets of the parties involved and see if they have any recovery capacity.

Appraisal Fraud and Cost-Benefit Analysis

The same scenario occurs in appraisal fraud. The industry depends on a local appraiser to place a value on that piece of property, and if they miss dramatically through negligence or outright fraud, they devalue it or give it greater value than what it is worth. For example, a house is appraised for $300,000 and it is worth $100,000. Within six months it's in early payment default and has been pushed right back down. The parties go after the appraiser. The appraiser does not have the resources to absorb a $200,000 hit, especially if it is fraud that is not covered by insurance. If a notary fails to do his or her job and allows fraud to occur by notarizing an instrument with a forged signature; the value of the fraudulent transaction will likely exceed the limits of their bond. To structure an effective settlement, you have to be able to define a win-win for the client. You can get a judgment for $300,000 against a notary knowing that you will only have a paper judgment. But on the flip side, that individual will never be a notary again. The question is whether the client wants to spend the legal fees on top of a $300,000 loss.

Alternative Dispute Resolution

We will occasionally use alternative dispute resolution (ADR) once the matter is filed and a TRO or complaint has been filed. If it is done through an attorney general's office or through a state agency, we will reach out to the potential fraudster or their counsel. That is when ADR can occur—usually a mediation, but in my experience, if there is only one party, you can settle it without going to mediation, especially when fraud is involved. The fraudulent party wants to protect its license or reputation in the industry. However, if there are multiple parties, with one or two really bad actors and with two more complicit parties, mediation will be pushed by the lesser offending parties. Mediation enables you to gather additional information for yourself. In other words, you can sit down with the entities that were not directly involved, get their explanation about the case, and offer to let them settle for a lesser amount. That refocuses your target and enables you to recoup some funds for your client. In some instances, the client may make a decision at that point to present the case to the authorities. In other cases, the client may decide to provide you with a war chest (the "settlement funds" from the lesser offending parties) and continue to pursue fraud charges against the bad actors. Fraud cases for mortgage clients are difficult because in this real estate environment, real estate values are already decreasing. Entities that at one point in time had a lot of liquidity and assets are heavily encumbered, and that factors into the cost benefit analysis.

Cost Reduction Strategies

We have leveraged technology to manage and reduce costs. A fraud case is more than likely going to involve people in multiple geographic locations across the country. Placing all the information available to the client on a secure extranet site enables them to access the information, and for you to have multiple points of perspective—whether from identity theft or loss mitigation. Many areas have online dockets and pleadings that enable you to run a name search on a company or entity nationwide to check for aliases or names. Knowledge is power in the fraud game, and when you are able to leverage technology to increase your knowledge with regard to the fraud scheme itself, you become an effective advocate for your client. You are able to combat and eradicate the fraud, and move to some type of recovery and final resolution of the matter.

Leveraging Prior Successes

Fraud is in every state, county/parish, and city. The ability to understand and view a problem nationally and then be able to attack it locally has great benefit to clients. We may have two to three fraud cases hit in one month, and we are able to leverage what we did in a prior case. Getting TROs in similar situations gives you credibility. We may be in Texas one day, Michigan later that week, and then Florida the next month. The ability to show different jurisdictions and different judges what we have done previously gives that judge some comfort that they can rely on the documents and theories presented to them. Always remember that TROs are an extraordinary remedy and can be difficult to obtain even in the most clear-cut fraud situations. On more than one occasion we argued for a TRO one afternoon, had the judge explain their concerns and what other documentation they would ideally prefer, and continuing the hearing until the next day. Then we go back to the client and work all night in pulling additional documentation and reworking our pleadings based on the additional information/documentation and then go right back in the next morning in front of the same judge for the TRO.

Analyzing Documents for Evidence of Fraud

If you are in the fraud practice, much of your success is based on experience. Each fraud file teaches you something new and useful for the next case, and you begin to build an experience base with a fraud team. One of the most important types of skills is to analyze documents. For example, in a fraud case, a critical document is the HUD-1 form. That enables you to ensure that all the "ins and outs" of the money are properly documented. Bank documents are critical, too. If you can demonstrate the wire transfer going in and then going out, that is hard evidence in court or at a settlement conference. Fraud, especially in the real estate industry, is an evolving process because origination products have evolved. The more you work at it, the better you become at it. You are able to spot issues and trends quickly, and be proactive about eradicating the fraud.

Conclusion

In the next year, I believe that we will see more servicing fraud. In the loan modification environment, many people who get into trial loan modifications and then permanent loan modifications ultimately fail. GSEs (Government-Sponsored Enterprise—Fannie Mae and Freddie Mac) are moving toward allowing less documentation in some of their loan modifications due to public and political pressure to move more defaulting homeowners into loan modifications. Less documentation is going to increase the potential for fraud. The way money changes hands and loans are originated will always be a target for fraud. In addition, we will likely continue to see more fraud in land title records as the system is fundamentally based on trust and has little preventive protection in place— usually as long as someone is willing to pay the filing fee they can easily record a fraudulent document that either alters the security instrument or fraudulently conveys the underlying property.

An attorney must be diligent, and as we continue to move through the current default/foreclosure crisis, we are going to see more fraud exist in this area for the next year or two. Hopefully, the industry will begin to see some semblance of greater recovery in 2012 and 2013, and with it will be a movement to get back to origination fraud. Knowing where the fraud occurred inside the transaction itself requires knowing and understanding the documents with which you are working. There are many times when you will see conflicting information: the borrower called in and gave inaccurate information or information that was contrary to what they said previously. You need to have a strong understanding of the documents and provide your client with accurate and realistic expectations as to what can happen at the end of the case. In some fraud cases, you will hit a big win and recover everything. However, in this environment, you are going to be chasing after a recovery. Set the client's expectations: the goal is to understand the fraud, determine where it originated, eradicate it to the extent possible, and conduct a cost/benefit analysis to determine whether to proceed with a civil lawsuit or turn the case over to the authorities. Develop a strong relationship with the federal, state, or local level law enforcement authorities. You are not an agent of the state, but you must ensure that they know your clients are good corporate citizens. The authorities are motivated to prosecute the bad actors and remove them from the industry. Know your documents, manage your client expectations, understand that there is both a civil and criminal side to mortgage fraud, and recognize when it is in your client's best interest to make a strategic change.

Key Takeaways

- Set the client's expectations: the goal is to understand the fraud, determine where it originated, eradicate it to the extent possible, and conduct a cost/benefit analysis to determine whether to proceed with a civil lawsuit or turn the case over to the authorities.
- If you discover fraud, analyze the situation based on the all the available information, if it is an ongoing fraud try to stop it immediately with a TRO, then engage in expedited discovery: request bank documents, checking accounts, and wire transfers; and begin to track the money as it moves through the fraudulent process.
- Establishing clear fraud is similar to reconstructing a puzzle: you have to find all of the pieces to construct the case. Use origination

files, check bank documents, and interview any witnesses who were involved.

- Use mediation to speak with complicit, but less involved actors in complex cases and gather information that will help your client. This enables you to gather additional information for yourself. You can sit down with the entities that were not directly involved, get their explanation about the case, and offer to let them settle for a lesser amount.

Robert Maddox is a partner at Bradley Arant Boult Cummings LLP. His practice focuses on financial services litigation with an emphasis on mortgage litigation and compliance and commercial/real estate litigation. Mr. Maddox is a certified mortgage banker and is one of only a handful of attorneys in the nation who have achieved this status. His national practice focuses primarily on representing two specific industries: financial institutions and mortgage companies. His representation of clients in the financial institutions and mortgage industry is both trial practice and compliance. The trial practice has led him to trial and appellate courts in over forty different states. He has handled matters both at the pre-litigation and initial complaint filing phase, as well as being employed during discovery, to depose expert witnesses, and at the pre-trial phase to assist the current counsel. On the compliance side, he has worked with both legal and business managers for multiple clients to draft and outline procedures in response to pending or new legislation.

Mr. Maddox earned his B.A. and M.A. both from the University of Alabama at Birmingham, and his J.D. from the Cumberland School of Law at Samford University. He is a member of the state bars of Alabama, Georgia, the District of Columbia, Tennessee, Texas, and New York.

Perspectives on Evaluating and Proceeding in a Fraud Case

Stephanie E. Kaiser

Partner

McGinnis, Lochridge & Kilgore LLP

ASPATORE

Introduction

My practice focuses on commercial litigation. I represent creditors in and out of litigation and bankruptcy. The number of cases on which I have worked that involve defaults and fraud have increased dramatically over the years. In those cases, I typically represent creditors, including farm credit system institutions and commercial lenders.

When I receive a case that involves fraud, I am sure to learn not only the details of the alleged fraud but also review the entire scope of the business involved. In most of the cases I have seen, the business accused of engaging in fraud did not necessarily begin its operation in a fraudulent manner. Often times, fraud occurred after a decline in the economy, the industry, or due to personal circumstances. Accordingly, it is important to consider not only the alleged fraudulent behavior but also the behavior and activity that existed before the alleged fraud began for patterns of behavior and possible motives. If the business operated in a fraudulent manner or engaged in fraud at the outset, then it is important to evaluate the business's affiliates or the key persons in the business in an attempt to unearth the origin and basis of the fraud.

This chapter summarizes some of the experiences I have had in working on fraud cases over the years and provides some practical tips in handling such cases.

Overview of Mortgage and Finance Fraud

I have been retained in numerous fraud cases on behalf of the creditor or defrauded party. Generally, my clients seek monetary and injunctive relief. In response to creditors' claims, some borrowers allege counterclaims to avoid liability under the notes or mortgages. If there was an underlying issue that precluded summary judgment, the lender and borrower were sometimes able to settle for an amount payable to the lender, but less than the actual debt owed as the cost benefit analysis of defending against the borrower's claims warranted settling for less than the actual debt. However, in other cases, the lender has maintained its claim and proceeded to judgment. The effect of a claim by a borrower is largely dictated by the: (1) the facts; and/or (2) exposure the claim has or may have on the portfolio.

Impact of the Economic Crisis

I have attributed much of the increase in mortgage and bank fraud cases to the economic crisis. Due to the economic downturn, many businesses have been unable to operate profitably and/or maintain their margins or ratios on their loans, resulting in monetary and/or non-monetary defaults. To avoid the discovery of the default, borrowers have submitted false financial information and/or engaged in other forms of fraud. For example, borrowers have inflated the costs or number of goods, converted loan proceeds (e.g., used the proceeds from one loan to pay another creditor), stored goods of third parties and held them out as their own during inspections, and/or engaged in check kites. Borrowers have also pledged their collateral for other debts contrary to loan instruments and/or transferred their non-exempt property to avoid the reach of creditors. As a result, the lender is left under-secured or unsecured.

In response to these efforts by borrowers, lenders have often increased the number of inspections they perform, required the borrowers to submit audited financials on a more frequent basis, and reduced the terms of their notes, among other things. However, there is no fail proof way to protect or ensure against fraud; and, with greater controls, come greater costs to service the loan. For example, lenders are required to spend more time inspecting collateral, requesting more financial information and/or more frequent updates on financial information, and auditing and reviewing the financial information received from the borrowers. And, despite these controls, if a borrower is inclined to engage in fraud, then the borrower will become familiar with whatever restrictions are placed on it by the lender and then find a way around the limitations. For example, a borrower may store collateral for a third party and then hold it out as its own during an inspection and may reflect such collateral on its financial statements. The lender would think that the borrower has complied with the collateral margin requirements and the loan is well secured when, in reality, it is not. The borrower could manipulate the cost of goods to indicate that it has complied with its margins. In short, lenders need to have controls in place to monitor compliance with the loan; however, controls do not guarantee compliance, and compliance does not always reflect a lack of fraud.

Authorities Used in Fraud Cases

In civil fraud cases, I have often alleged claims for breach of contract, conversion, and common law fraud, as well as claims under Texas Uniform Fraudulent Transfer Act (TUFTA) and the Texas Theft Liability Act, and pursued applications for injunctive relief and sequestrations of property. *See, e.g.,* TEX. BUS. & COM. CODE §§ 24.001, *et seq.*; TEX. CIV. PRAC. & REM. CODE §§ 134.001, *et seq.*; TEX. R. CIV. P. 680-683 & 696-708; TEX. CIV. PRAC. & REM. CODE §§ 62.001, *et seq.* & 65.001, *et seq.* When required and/or appropriate to do so, criminal referrals to the FBI, the U.S. Attorneys' Office, the District Attorneys' Office, and/or other relevant government agencies have also been made. *See, e.g.,* 12 C.F.R. §§ 612.2300, *et seq.* and 18 U.S.C. §§ 658 and 1014.

Trends in Fraud Schemes

In my experience, lenders are generally able to identify misrepresentations and the actions identified herein. However, such actions and/or misrepresentations may not be discovered unless and until the borrowers run out of options and/or default under the loan. For example, many of the cases on which I have worked involved borrowers who have:

1. misrepresented their finances to obtain loans and/or maintain compliance under loans
2. destroyed financial records to conceal defaults and/or misrepresentations concerning their finances
3. engaged in check kites and/or conversion
4. transferred property to others in order to avoid creditors' reach, secure other debt obligations, and/or satisfy other debts

In my experience, some of these actions are more common because they:

1. are easier to commit
2. provide an immediate solution to a perceived short-term problem
3. sometimes lack immediate transparency

Borrowers may also engage in these actions because they perceive that there are few alternatives. For example, borrowers may avoid filing for bankruptcy relief to avoid a criminal referral and/or because fraudulent transfers and/or preferences can be struck in bankruptcy. If borrowers engage in the fraudulent actions described above, then it is often because they believe such actions will buy them time to find a legitimate solution to their financial problems or for the economy to turn around and/or to wait out the limitations period applicable to such actions.

Federal and State Regulations

Fraud has become more commonplace in recent years, and the means of addressing fraud seem to be more available. For example, in state and federal courts in Texas, it is not uncommon to obtain injunctive relief to preserve information or assets and to sequester property that serves as collateral for a loan. Criminal referrals may also be made in connection with bankruptcy cases and in connection with fraud relating to farm credit system institutions, for example. Courts also appear to appreciate the need to obtain discovery in a more expeditious manner and the complexities that may be involved in obtaining electronically stored information, such as e-mails and documents saved on a hard drive. Spoliation instructions also appear more common and prove important in fraud cases. In general, courts appear to recognize that fraud is occurring more frequently and that defrauded parties should be protected when possible to prevent further harm. If borrowers who engage in fraud know their actions are subject to discovery and subject to spoliation instructions, then such borrowers may be less likely to engage in fraudulent activity.

Although discovery may be more accessible, it is also costly. Because fraud is often complex (and hidden by design), discovering fraud and engaging in tracing analysis generally proves expensive and, sometimes, cost prohibitive. The role of the government may be an important one as the government can engage in the discovery more cost effectively; however, due to backlog and strained resources, the government may not conclude their investigation and/or handling of case until years after it begins. Civil cases generally take a fraction of the time (although civil cases involving fraud generally take twelve to twenty-four months before a judgment or other resolution is made).

For example, I represented a minority shareholder and limited partner, as the plaintiff, in a check kite case. The plaintiff's business partner managed the businesses at issue and engaged in a check kite at more than one bank. One of the banks had fraud detection software that alerted the bank to a possible check kite. The bank did not close down the account when it received the notifications; instead, the account remained open for a period of time, and the check kite continued. Toward the end of the kite, calculations were made as to the float time and the number of days needed to be made whole. After the time period passed, the check kite was shut down and was pushed on a smaller bank. The plaintiff sustained the loss as a guarantor on a loan at the smaller bank. The plaintiff filed suit against the business partner and the bank that was notified of the possible kite activity. A forensic accountant was used in that case to track the kite and testify about the parties' involvement in the kite. A bank expert was retained to testify about policies and procedures regarding bank fraud and the software employed by the bank to detect the kite. A jury awarded damages in favor of my client and against the business partner and bank. That case was on the docket for a number of years, and sentencing has not yet occurred with regard to the business partner who engaged in the check kite (the bank was not prosecuted).

Litigation Strategies for Countering Allegations

Common Claims against Lenders

In my experience, borrowers allege claims against lenders mainly in an attempt to reduce their debt to the lender. It is possible to have a bad loan or set of loan documents that cause harm to the borrower. However, generally that issue will not come to light unless and until a borrower defaults. When a borrower defaults and retains counsel, the borrower will evaluate possible claims against the lender to offset the borrower's liability to the lender. Because the lender will have advanced the funds by the time of the default, it is generally not an issue of whether the lender should be repaid but what amount the lender should be repaid and/or whether the borrower's acts or omissions constituted a default in the first place. For example, in the event the loan should never have been made due to fraud by the lender, then the borrower's remedy, in Texas, would include the right to rescind the agreement. If the borrower rescinded the agreement, then the borrower would have to return to the lender any monies the borrower received from the lender and/or offset any such amounts by any damages the borrower sustained because of the fraud. I, therefore, have not been involved in many cases where a counter-claim alleged against a lender proceeded to a final judgment.

Lenders' Responses to Claims

Although counter-claims against lenders do not always proceed to judgment, claims by borrowers have increased over the last twelve to thirty-six months because of the economy. With more breaches and suits, claims by borrowers have increased in an attempt to offset the debt owed to the lender by the borrower. When a claim is made against a lender, it is important to evaluate the claim not only in light of the borrower(s) at issue but also with regard to the lender's portfolio. The lender can then determine how it wants to respond to the claim (e.g., whether it wants to defend against the claim, obtain a declaratory judgment on the issue, or settle).

Structuring the Litigation Strategy

Although each case is different and should be evaluated accordingly, it is important to:

1. Evaluate the loan documents, payment history, the financials, and the parties' communications, e.g., to get a sense of what happened and when;

2. Ensure that the proper notices have gone out and that all conditions precedent to litigation have been satisfied or waived (if not, then ensure that such notices are provided prior to suit as provided by law);

3. Draft a petition and an application for a sequestration and/or injunctive relief if there is an emergency or a threat to collateral;

4. Request financial documents and other discoverable items from the borrower and determine if it is necessary to copy the hard drives of any computer used by the borrower;

5. Gather all of the bank and financial-related records and determine if a forensic accountant should be retained to reconstruct the fraud and/or to perform a tracing analysis; and

6. Gather all other relevant information and determine the best option for proceeding (e.g., judgment or other resolution).

Challenges to Discovery

The goal of the above strategy is to locate, gather, and protect the collateral or assets of the borrowers that may satisfy a judgment, to obtain a judgment on the relevant claims, and/or to protect the client's rights. Discovery is a challenge, especially with the use of computers and other electronic means because much of the information can be shredded, deleted, or otherwise compromised. If the collateral has been sold or wasted, then it is difficult, if not impossible, to get it back. Depending on the length of time in which the fraud took place, witnesses can be difficult to find, documents become more numerous to review (if they exist), and the task of figuring it all out becomes increasingly difficult. A computer forensics technologist can help resurrect damaged electronic information (if the computer exists and accounts to which the information may have been transferred are located). Bank records can be subpoenaed from the banking institution (often at significant cost) and tax returns can generally be subpoenaed from the accountant. Ultimately, the discovery of relevant information, obtaining cooperation from witnesses in light of the criminal implications that may be involved, and the cost of establishing liability and/or recovering from the fraud pose the greatest challenge.

Winning Litigation Practices

It is generally best to proceed as quickly as possible in the event of default and obtain all necessary information, including documents and electronic information, up front. As the suit progresses, obtaining additional material is important, as well. Establishing and controlling the case from the beginning can prove advantageous to lenders in the event of default and fraud. As indicated above, it may be important to retain an expert in computer forensics or accounting and review the available information in order to advise the lender on the available evidence, options for proceeding, and/or potential sources of recovery. Lenders need to understand the total debt exposure and the ability to recover in order to make an informed decision on how to proceed in the event of fraud.

Balancing Resolution and Litigation

In many cases, it is important to identify the default and initiate suit as soon as possible. In some cases, however, it is better to engage in informal discovery and negotiate a resolution outside of litigation (while observing and complying with any reporting requirements that may exist). Depending on the extent of the fraud, discovery can be cost prohibitive or make it difficult for a lender to maximize its recovery. In addition, depending on the venue, it may take a long time for a lender to obtain a judgment. If the lender is able to secure information up front that would allow it to make an informed decision on settlement, then a lender may desire to negotiate a resolution, if possible, as opposed to engaging in protracted litigation. However, with certain borrowers, a lender may be unable to rely on or trust the information it receives and litigation and/or bankruptcy may be the only way to force transparency.

Alternative Dispute Resolution as an Alternative to Litigation

Although litigating fraud is often expensive, litigation generally invites opportunities for resolution shy of trial. For example, mediation is often required when a suit is filed in Texas and is typically scheduled after discovery so that the parties can engage in meaningful discussions of the risks and benefits of proceeding to trial based on the information obtained. Although it is generally beneficial to engage in mediation after discovery has been conducted, some parties may choose to mediate at the beginning of the case if the facts are generally known. Doing so allows the parties to avoid costs associated with discovery. However, settling a case involving fraud must be thoughtfully considered to avoid waiver of possible claims. The factors to consider when settling a case include:

1. whether a suit was filed
2. the status of the litigation at the time of settlement
3. the information obtained during the litigation
4. the assets available for recovery and/or involved in the matter
5. the debt exposure
6. whether counterclaims have been alleged or could be alleged
7. re-finance opportunities
8. the cost of litigation

9. the potential for bankruptcy
10. the security position of the client
11. whether the borrowers engaged in any criminal activity

If possible and if appropriate, then a lender may also attempt to secure a judgment, an injunction, a forbearance agreement with an *ipso facto* clause tailored to the collateral, additional collateral, and payment in full.

A goal of engaging in alternative dispute resolution, such as mediation, is to present the parties with an opportunity to resolve the matters at issue prior to trial. If bankruptcy is a possibility, then it may be important to proceed to litigation if information can be obtained through discovery to preclude discharge. If bankruptcy can be avoided through settlement, and if the lender would recover less in the event of bankruptcy, then it may be important to settle. However, in many cases where fraud is involved, it is often better to proceed to bankruptcy as the process is more transparent and others can participate in the discovery process and the prosecution of the fraud. The participants will also share in the cost, but the trustee has certain powers that may allow for creditors to maximize recovery.

Conclusion

This chapter provides some tips and guidance when handling a fraud case, realizing that each case is unique and should be evaluated and treated as such. Fraud cases can be costly and can involve considerations that do not exist in the normal breach of contract or tort case. Litigators should confer with experts and experienced practitioners at the beginning of the matter to determine the best manner of proceeding in a particular case. Lawyers who represent borrowers who engage in fraud should be sure to advise their clients on spoliation, preservation of evidence, bankruptcy issues, and the possible need to retain criminal counsel. Generally, lawyers who represent borrowers who engage in fraud prefer to reach a resolution as quickly as possible to limit discovery and exposing other issues that may exist, whereas counsel for the lender may want to take some time to engage in formal or informal discovery before deciding on how to proceed or resolve a particular matter.

Advice for Practitioners

Because many fraud cases involve debt, bankruptcy is often involved. I would encourage trustees and debtors' counsel to investigate fraud and the papers filed by debtors in bankruptcy. Debtors' counsel should advise debtors on the possibility of criminal referrals and the consequences of engaging in fraudulent behavior in and out of bankruptcy. Bankruptcy can be a great venue for resolving bank fraud; however, if debtors are unaware of the process and the potential for a referral, then bankruptcy can be a waste of resources if the case is dismissed and/or improperly investigated.

Key Takeaways

- Evaluate each case on its own merit.
- Investigate the loan documents, bank statements, and business activities carefully.
- Determine what information is needed and gather or otherwise secure as expeditiously as possible any documents and information that may be at risk of spoliation.
- Gather information that will support an informed decision about options for proceeding, including settlement.
- Determine if experts should be retained early in the process to get guidance on how best to proceed.
- Proceed to bankruptcy when fraud is involved. The process is more transparent and other parties can participate in the prosecution of the fraud. If bankruptcy relief is sought, then investigate the documents filed by the debtor carefully.

Related Resources:

- TEX. R. CIV. P. 680-683.
- TEX. R. CIV. P. 696-708.
- TEX. BUS. & COM. CODE §§ 24.001, *et seq.*
- TEX. CIV. PRAC. & REM. CODE §§ 62.001, *et seq.*
- TEX. CIV. PRAC. & REM. CODE §§ 65.001, *et seq.*
- TEX. CIV. PRAC. & REM. CODE §§ 134.001, *et seq.*
- 12 C.F.R. §§ 612.2300, *et seq.*

- 18 U.S.C. §§ 658 and 1014.
- FCA Referral Form
- Sample Petition in a Fraud Suit

Stephanie E. Kaiser is a partner with McGinnis, Lochridge & Kilgore LLP. She is a trial lawyer who represents individuals and various business entities (both national and international) in a wide variety of civil litigation, bankruptcy, and administrative law matters, including various banking and financial service disputes in and out of bankruptcy, adversary proceedings, lease disputes, insurance coverage disputes, construction law matters, fraud cases, state board matters, and personal injury cases. She has represented clients in various industries and professions, including the farm credit system and other banking and financial service institutions, professional associations, and the leasing, insurance, health care (including medical and dental practitioners), alarm system, tower construction, and cable industries.

Ms. Kaiser has been recognized by Texas Law & Politics *as a "Texas Rising Star" in business litigation since 2006. She is a fellow of the Texas Bar Foundation and a member of the Austin Young Lawyers Association and the Austin Bar Association. She earned her B.A., summa cum laude, from Texas Christian University and her J.D. from the University of Texas School of Law.*

Dedication: *I would like to thank my clients, who have entrusted me with their work over the years, and my family, who has given me the opportunity to pursue my career.*

APPENDICES

APPENDIX A

SAMPLE EQUITABLE SUBROGATION PLEADING

I. THE FIRST MORTGAGE

1. On or about January 1, 2003, Borrower executed a mortgage for the benefit of First Lender (the "First Mortgage"). Among other things, the First Mortgage encumbered and constituted a lien on property located at Block 1, Lot 2 on the official Tax Map of City, commonly known as Property.

2. The First Mortgage was recorded in the Middlesex County Clerk's office on January 15, 2003 in Mortgage Book 1, Page 2.

3. On February 1, 2003, the Tax Collector of the City issued Tax Sale Certificate No. 03 in connection with delinquent taxes that were due to the City for the Property.

4. Tax Sale Certificate No. 03 was recorded in the Middlesex County Clerk's office on February 20, 2003 in Mortgage Book 1, Page 2.

5. Upon information and belief as to Second Lender's lien, the taxes owed on the Property constituted first-position liens.

II. THE SECOND MORTGAGE

6. On October 1, 2003, the Borrower gave an "Equity Source Account Mortgage" to Second Lender (the "Second Mortgage"). The Second Mortgage secured a $40,000 line of credit given by Second Lender to the Borrower pursuant to an "Equity Source Account Agreement and Disclosure" between Borrower and Second Lender (the "Second Lender Agreement").

7. The Second Mortgage was recorded in the County Clerk's office on January 15, 2004 at Mortgage Book 2, Page 2.

III. THE THIRD MORTGAGE

8. On or about January 16, 2004, the Borrower refinanced the Property (the "Refinance").

9. In connection with the Refinance, the Borrower obtained a loan from Third Lender in the amount of $150,000 (the "Third Lender

Loan"). The Third Lender Loan was secured by a mortgage given by the Borrower to Third Lender on January 16, 2004 in the amount of $150,000 (the "Third Mortgage").

10. The Third Mortgage was recorded in the Middlesex County Clerk's office on March 12, 2004 at Mortgage Book 2, Page 10.

IV. THE PAY-OFF OF THE PRIOR LIENS WITH THE PROCEEDS OF THE THIRD LENDER LOAN

11. In connection with the Refinance, $120,000 of the proceeds of the Third Lender Loan was used to payoff the First Mortgage on or about January 16, 2004. The pay-off funds were transferred by means of a check made payable to First Lender that was prepared and sent via UPS by the closing agent.

12. The First Mortgage was subsequently discharged by means of a Mortgage, Release, Satisfaction, and Discharge, dated January 27, 2004, which was recorded in the County Clerk's office on March 17, 2004 at Discharge Mortgage Book 1, Page 2.

13. In connection with the Refinance, $10,000 of the proceeds of the Third Lender were used to payoff Tax Sale Certificate No. 03. The pay-off funds were transferred by means of a check made payable to Collector, Township of City, that was prepared and sent via UPS by the closing agent.

14. Tax Sale Certificate No. 03-116 was subsequently cancelled of record on or about March 19, 2004, and recorded by the County Clerk.

15. In connection with the Refinance, $5,000 of the proceeds of the Third Lender Loan were used to payoff outstanding municipal taxes on the Property. The taxes owed on the Property constituted first-position liens. The pay-off funds were transferred by means of a check made payable to Collector, Township of City, that was prepared and sent via UPS by the closing agent.

16. The First Mortgage, taxes owed pursuant to Tax Sale Certificate No. 03 and taxes paid in connection with the Property each constituted liens on the Property superior in position to that of the Second Mortgage.

17. Third Lender did not know of the existence of the Second Mortgage at the time that the First Mortgage, Tax Sale Certificate No. 03-116 and taxes were paid off.

18. The first time Third Lender learned of the existence of the Second Mortgage was when it was served with the Complaint in this matter.

19. Second Lender will be unjustly enriched if it is allowed to foreclose on the Property without regard to the prior liens on the Property that were paid off with the proceeds of the Third Lender Loan, including the First Mortgage, Tax Sale Certificate No. 03 and other taxes paid on the Property.

20. As the proceeds of the Third Lender Loan were used to payoff the First Mortgage, Tax Sale Certificate No. 03 and, upon information and belief, other taxes paid on the Property, Third Lender stands in the shoes of the lien holders that it paid off and is entitled to priority position over the Second Mortgage to the extent of the amount of those liens.

WHEREFORE, Third Lender demands judgment against Second Lender declaring that, by virtue of the doctrine of equitable subrogation, that Third Lender holds a priority position on the Property superior to that of the Second Mortgage to the extent that liens prior to the Second Mortgage were paid off, and awarding attorneys' fees, costs of suit, and such other relief as this Court deems just and equitable.

Courtesy of Michael R. O'Donnell, Riker Danzig Scherer Hyland & Perretti LLP

APPENDIX B

SAMPLE EQUITABLE LIEN/MORTGAGE AND REFORMATION NUNC PRO TUNC PLEADING

1. On or about April 1, 2009, Lender made a loan to Borrower, in the principal sum of $500,000 (the "$500,000 Loan").

2. On or about April 1, 2009, to evidence the $500,000 Loan, Defendant, as an officer of Borrower and on behalf of Borrower, executed and delivered to Lender a Promissory Note in the original principal amount of $500,000 ($500,000 Note").

3. Pursuant to the $500,000 Note, interest on the $500,000 Loan accrued at a variable initial rate of seven point seven five percent (7.75%) per annum. The $500,000 Note is payable in (i) three hundred (300) consecutive monthly installments of principal and interest in the amount of $2,680.80 commencing on May 1, 2009 and thereafter on the first (1st) day of each succeeding calendar month, and (ii) a balloon payment of all outstanding principal and accrued interest due on April 1, 2039.

4. Pursuant to the terms of the $500,000 Note, Borrower is required to pay a late charge equal to five percent (5%) of any payment that Lender does not receive within ten (10) calendar days of its due date thereunder.

5. Also, pursuant to the terms of the $500,000 Note, Borrower agreed to Lender's costs and expenses, including but not limited to attorneys' fees, in connection with enforcing its rights under the $500,000 Note and the Borrower Mortgage (as defined below).

6. On or about April 1, 2009, Borrower executed and delivered to Lender, as collateral security for Borrower's obligations under the Loan Documents, including the $500,000 Loan, a Mortgage ("Borrower Mortgage"), pursuant to which Borrower granted to Lender a second-lien mortgage on the real property located at 1 Valley Street, Orange, New Jersey 07079 (the "Mortgaged Premises"). Upon information and belief, the Mortgaged Premises is a commercial property.

7. However, at the time of the commencement of this foreclosure action, Lender discovered that the Mortgaged Premises, in fact, was not owned by Borrower. At the time of the closing of the $500,000 Loan, the

Mortgaged Premises was purchased by Defendant, individually, as opposed to the Borrower of which the Defendant is the sole principal.

8. The Borrower Mortgage was recorded on April 10, 2009, in the County Clerk's office in Mortgage Book 100, page 1, and is revealed by a title search with respect to the Mortgaged Premises.

9. At all relevant times, Lender intended and contractually agreed to receive a mortgage lien as collateral security for the $500,000 Loan, as evidenced by the Borrower Mortgage.

10. Defendant obtained the benefit and use of the proceeds of the $500,000 Loan and ownership of the Mortgaged Premises free of record lien in favor of Lender.

Wherefore, Lender respectfully requests that this Court enter judgment against Defendant for the following relief:

a. adjudging that Lender has an equitable mortgage lien nunc pro tunc until date of closing (April 1, 2010) on the Mortgaged Premises;

b. directing that Lender be paid the amount due on the Borrower Mortgage together with interest and costs; and

c. such other relief as the Court may deem to be just, proper and equitable.

Courtesy of Michael R. O'Donnell, Riker Danzig Scherer Hyland & Perretti LLP

APPENDIX C

IN RE PLAZA MORTGAGE AND FINANCE CORP.

United States Bankruptcy Court,
N.D. Georgia,
Atlanta Division.

In re PLAZA MORTGAGE AND FINANCE CORPORATION, Debtor.
Neil C. GORDON, Trustee in Bankruptcy of the Estate of Plaza Mortgage and Finance Corporation, Plaintiff,

v.

Martin BASROON; Joseph Girardot; Leslie Johnson; Fred Kaunitz; Nathan Pasha; Ferraro, Wood & Company f/k/a Ferraro, Gensib and Wood f/k/a Saltiel, Basroon, Ferraro, Gensib and Wood f/k/a Saltiel, Basroon and Ferraro; Michael R. Ferraro; Carl D. Gensib; James M. Wood; Rhea Basroon; Ida Basroon; Jody Basroon; and Andrew Basroon, Defendants.

Bankruptcy No. A93-65102-JB.

Adv. No. 94-6068.

Aug. 28, 1995.

Chapter 11 trustee sued debtor's former accountants for malpractice and fraud arising out of operation of debtor as "Ponzi" or pyramid scheme. Accountants moved to dismiss, arguing lack of standing and doctrine of in pari delicto. The Bankruptcy Court, Joyce Bihary, J., held that: (1) Chapter 11 trustee had standing to sue accountants for fraud and malpractice on behalf of debtor; (2) damages would be better calculated by reference to monies improperly used by president of debtor who was also member of accounting firm, accounting fees paid, and other accepted methods of measuring damages, rather than by difference between amount invested and assets on hand; and (3) counsel were required to supplement record and brief additional issues before court could rule on accountants' motion to dismiss based on in pari delicto doctrine.

So ordered.

West Headnotes

[1] Bankruptcy 51 2154.1

51 Bankruptcy
51II Courts; Proceedings in General
51II(B) Actions and Proceedings in General
51k2154 Rights of Action by or on Behalf of Trustee or Debtor
51k2154.1 k. In general; standing.

Chapter 11 trustee had standing to sue Chapter 11 debtor's former accountants for malpractice and fraud arising out of operation of debtor as "Ponzi" or pyramid scheme; however, method of measuring damages had to be refined and trustee was required to clarify elements of damages claimed. Bankr.Code, 11 U.S.C.A. § 541(a)(1).

[2] Bankruptcy 51 2159.1

51 Bankruptcy
51II Courts; Proceedings in General
51II(B) Actions and Proceedings in General
51k2159 Parties
51k2159.1 k. In general.

Standing is jurisdictional in nature, and whether plaintiff has standing is threshold inquiry.

[3] Bankruptcy 51 2001

51 Bankruptcy
51I In General
51I(A) In General
51k2001 k. In general.

Bankruptcy is collective debt collection device.

[4] Bankruptcy 51 3008.1

51 Bankruptcy
51VIII Trustees
51k3008 Powers, Duties and Fiduciary Capacity
51k3008.1 k. In general.

Trustee's job is to investigate debtor's financial affairs, liquidate assets, pursue debtor's causes of action, and acquire assets through avoiding powers in order to make distribution to creditors.

[5] Bankruptcy 51 2154.1

51 Bankruptcy
51II Courts; Proceedings in General
51II(B) Actions and Proceedings in General
51k2154 Rights of Action by or on Behalf of Trustee or Debtor
51k2154.1 k. In general; standing.

Removal of assets through operation of debtor as "Ponzi" scheme caused damage to debtor, and thus, trustee had standing to sue debtor's former accountants for this type of injury.

[6] Accountants 11A 10.1

11A Accountants
11Ak10 Actions
11Ak10.1 k. In general.

Accountants 11A 11

11A Accountants
11Ak10 Actions
11Ak11 k. Damages.

In Chapter 11 trustee's action against debtor's former accountants for malpractice and fraud arising out of the operation of debtor as "Ponzi" or pyramid scheme, damages would be better calculated by reference to monies improperly used by accountant, who was also president of debtor, accounting fees paid, and other accepted methods of measuring damages, rather than by difference between amount invested and assets on hand; thus, trustee was required to file pleading containing separate statement for each item of damage claimed against accountants, brief description of item of damage, dollar amount claim, and citation to law, rule, regulation, or any decision authorizing recovery for that particular item of damage.

[7] Accountants 11A 10.1

11A Accountants
11Ak10 Actions
11Ak10.1 k. In general.

Bankruptcy trustee, in pleading claim against third party participant in "Ponzi" scheme, should be careful to plead claims belonging to debtor and injury to debtor in order to survive motion to dismiss; trustee should be careful not to plead for recovery based on any injury to investor/creditors, even though fraud on investors will be part of background allegations.

[8] Accountants 11A 10.1

11A Accountants
11Ak10 Actions
11Ak10.1 k. In general.

Bankruptcy trustee, in pleading claim against third party participant in "Ponzi" scheme, should be careful not to plead damages as amount equal to funds invested in debtor's "Ponzi" scheme, but should measure damages based on funds improperly paid out by debtor in order to survive motion to dismiss.

[9] Corporations 101 428(11)

101 Corporations
101XI Corporate Powers and Liabilities
101XI(B) Representation of Corporation by Officers and Agents
101k428 Notice to Officer or Agent as Affecting Corporation
101k428(11) k. Officer interested adversely.

Adverse interest exception is exception to general rule that corporation is charged with constructive knowledge of all material facts of which its officers or agents acquire knowledge.

[10] Corporations 101 432(1)

101 Corporations
101XI Corporate Powers and Liabilities
101XI(B) Representation of Corporation by Officers and Agents
101k432 Evidence as to Authority
101k432(1) k. Presumptions as to authority in general.

Where officer or agent of corporation is engaged in scheme to defraud corporation, presumption that knowledge held by agent was disclosed to corporation fails because he cannot be presumed to have disclosed that which would expose and defeat his fraudulent purpose.

[11] Corporations 101 428(11)

101 Corporations
101XI Corporate Powers and Liabilities
101XI(B) Representation of Corporation by Officers and Agents
101k428 Notice to Officer or Agent as Affecting Corporation
101k428(11) k. Officer interested adversely.

Sole representative or sole actor doctrine is exception to adverse interest exception to general rule that corporation is charged with constructive knowledge of all material facts of which its officers or agents acquire knowledge.

[12] Corporations 101 428(11)

101 Corporations
101XI Corporate Powers and Liabilities
101XI(B) Representation of Corporation by Officers and Agents
101k428 Notice to Officer or Agent as Affecting Corporation
101k428(11) k. Officer interested adversely.

In cases where business or transaction in question is entrusted to officer or agent of corporation as its sole representative, adverse interest exception does not apply and knowledge of officer or agent is imputable to corporation; reason for rule is that, where officer in question is sole representative of that corporation, there is no one to whom to impart his knowledge and no one from whom he may conceal it.

[13] Federal Courts 170B 414

170B Federal Courts
170BVI State Laws as Rules of Decision
170BVI(C) Application to Particular Matters
170Bk414 k. Corporations and associations; banks and trust companies; securities.

State law, not federal law, governs imputation of knowledge to corporate victims of alleged negligence.
Larry H. Chesin, Kirwan, Parks, Chesin & Pemar, Atlanta, GA, for plaintiff.

Robert M. Finlayson, II, Mozley, Finlayson & Loggins, Atlanta, GA, for defendants.

ORDER

JOYCE BIHARY, Bankruptcy Judge.

In this case, the Court must decide whether the trustee has standing to sue the debtor's former accountants for malpractice and fraud where the debtor was operated as a "Ponzi" or pyramid scheme and where the debtor's president and one of its shareholders was a partner in the defendant accounting firms. This case also involves the issue of whether the trustee's claims are barred by the doctrine of *in pari delicto* as a result of the wrongful acts of the debtor.

Procedurally, this adversary proceeding is before the Court on two motions filed by Defendants Ferraro, Wood & Company, James M. Wood, Carl D. Gensib, and Michael R. Ferraro (the "Accountant Defendants" or "defendants"):

(1) a motion styled "Second Motion to Dismiss This Adversary Proceeding and/or Motion for Summary Judgment" (the "Standing Motion"); and

(2) a motion styled "Partial Summary Judgment on Issue of Statutes of Limitations" (the "Statute of Limitations Motion").

The main bankruptcy case was commenced by an involuntary petition on April 5, 1993. At the time the petition was filed, a state receivership action was pending in the Superior Court of Fulton County. After a contested hearing, this Court entered an Order for relief under Chapter 11 on June 2, 1993 and appointed a Chapter 11 Trustee.

The Debtor Plaza Mortgage and Finance Corporation ("Plaza") was, prior to the commencement of the bankruptcy case, engaged in the business of providing mortgage financing to higher than normal credit risk borrowers. For purposes of the pending motions, the parties do not dispute that Plaza obtained the funds to make its loans from investors, to whom it promised very high rates of return. After Defendant Martin Basroon became president of Plaza in September of 1988, Plaza was run as a largely fraudulent enterprise, organized as a Ponzi scheme.[FN1] Plaza remained in business not on the basis of earnings from loans made to borrowers, but on the basis of money received from new investors.

> FN1. A description of the term "Ponzi scheme" and the historical background of the term are fully discussed in *Merrill v. Abbott (In re Independent Clearing House Co.)*, 41 B.R. 985, 994 n. 12 (Bankr.D.Utah 1984), *aff'd in part, rev'd in part, Merrill v. Dietz (In re Universal Clearing House Co.)*, 62 B.R. 118 (D.Utah 1986).

In this adversary proceeding, the trustee has asserted claims against a number of defendants including Plaza's former president, Martin Basroon (both in his capacity as an officer of Plaza and in his capacity as a partner in the defendant accounting firms which performed work for Plaza), Plaza's former attorney, a former employee of Plaza, one of Plaza's founding shareholders, the accounting firms used by Plaza, and the partners of those accounting firms. [FN2] All of the defendants are alleged to have participated with the debtor in the Ponzi scheme.

FN2. The Court has already entered a judgment as to liability on all claims asserted in the complaint against Mr. Basroon.

The complaint contains many allegations as to all defendants and separate allegations and claims as to each defendant. With respect to the Accountant Defendants, the trustee contends that Plaza suffered injury as a result of the accountants' negligence and as a result of Basroon's fraud as an accountant. The trustee has alleged, *inter alia*, that the accountants were hopelessly negligent in failing to implement any controls or supervisory procedures to prevent mistakes or fraud.

In the Standing Motion, the Accountant Defendants argue that the trustee lacks any standing to bring the claims asserted against the Accountant Defendants, as these claims really belong to the investors. Alternatively, defendants argue that if the trustee has any claims, they are barred as a matter of law by the doctrine of *in pari delicto*.

I. The Standing Argument

[1] The case law is well-established that a trustee in bankruptcy lacks standing to assert claims on behalf of investors/creditors of a debtor as opposed to claims belonging to the debtor. *Caplin v. Marine Midland Grace Trust Co. of New York*, 406 U.S. 416, 92 S.Ct. 1678, 32 L.Ed.2d 195 (1972); *E.F. Hutton & Co. Inc. v. Hadley*, 901 F.2d 979 (11th Cir.1990); *Williams v. California 1st Bank*, 859 F.2d 664 (9th Cir.1988). It is also clear that causes of action belonging to the debtor are included as property of the estate under 11 U.S.C. § 541(a)(1) and may be asserted by the trustee. Here, the trustee maintains that his claims are asserted on behalf of the debtor and are for injuries to the debtor due to the accountants' negligence and Defendant Martin Basroon's fraud. Defendants respond by arguing that the claims are "really" brought on behalf of the investors/creditors, citing a number of cases dismissing claims asserted by trustees against alleged participants in Ponzi schemes.

[2] Standing is jurisdictional in nature, and whether plaintiff has standing is a threshold inquiry. *E.F. Hutton*, 901 F.2d at 983. The cases cited by Defendants show that it is difficult for a trustee in bankruptcy to maintain a claim against a third party who participated with the debtor in defrauding

creditors. The starting point for analyzing a trustee's standing here is the 1972 Supreme Court case of *Caplin v. Marine Midland Grace Trust Co.* In *Caplin,* the Supreme Court held that a trustee in a reorganization under Chapter X of the Bankruptcy Act did not have standing to assert, on behalf of persons holding debentures issued by the debtor, claims of misconduct by an indenture trustee. *Caplin* was a five-to-four decision and the Court noted that the issue was "a difficult one" and has caused "even the most able jurists to disagree." *Caplin,* 406 U.S. at 421-22, 92 S.Ct. at 1682. Deciding that the trustee in a reorganization lacked standing, the Court found that nowhere in the statutory scheme of the Bankruptcy Act or the Trust Indenture Act of 1939 was there a suggestion that the trustee in a reorganization was to assume the responsibility of suing third parties on behalf of debenture holders. Second, the trustee in *Caplin* did not argue that the debtor had any claim against the indenture trustee and the "conspicuous silence on this point is a tacit admission that no such claim could be made." *Id.* at 429, 92 S.Ct. at 1686. Third, the Court held that a suit by the trustee may be inconsistent with independent actions by debenture holders.

In *Williams* and *E.F. Hutton,* the Ninth and Eleventh Circuits found the trustees in bankruptcy lacked standing to sue third parties who participated with the debtors in Ponzi schemes. Both courts found it significant that when Congress rewrote the bankruptcy laws in 1978, it considered and rejected a provision which would have overruled *Caplin.* However, in both of these cases, the trustees were clearly asserting claims belonging to creditors, and not claims belonging to the debtor. In *Williams,* the trustee had taken an assignment of creditors' claims, and the court found the debtor had no claim of its own against the defendant bank. In *E.F. Hutton,* the trustee conceded he was asserting claims of customer creditors rather than the debtor entity. The court also stated: "We emphasize that our holding is restricted to the specific facts in this case." *E.F. Hutton,* 901 F.2d at 985.

Defendants rely on *Feltman v. Prudential Bache Sec.,* 122 B.R. 466 (S.D.Fla.1990), a case in which the trustee alleged that the debtor had been injured, but the court still dismissed the trustee's claims for lack of standing. The rationale in *Feltman,* however, is not particularly compelling here. There, the Chapter 11 trustee and the unsecured creditors committee of two corporate debtors sued a brokerage house, bankers, and accountants that defrauded investors in a massive embezzlement scheme. The trustee alleged that the debtors were injured by defendants' fraud and by their allowing the debtor to continue in business past the point of insolvency.[FN3] Holding that the trustee could not assert claims based on injury to the debtor corporations, the court found the debtor corporations could not be injured, because they were "sham" corporations. Thus, the court concluded "any alleged injury to the debtors is as illusory as was their corporate identity." *Id.* at 474. Here, there is no allegation that Plaza was a sham corporation. Furthermore, the result is troublesome if it means that the bankruptcy process is of no utility for creditors of Ponzi scheme debtors. Under the *Feltman* reasoning, in such a case the trustee's hands are tied and each creditor is on his or her own.

> FN3. In *Feltman,* the trustee also tried to assert claims on behalf of specific creditors and on behalf of creditors in general. Following *Caplin,* the court found that the trustee had no standing to raise claims based on specific creditors' interests. Regarding the allegations that the claims were brought on behalf of all creditors, the court found that plaintiffs failed to show such claims would belong to creditors in general outside of bankruptcy.

The other reason given in *Feltman* for dismissing the trustee's claims was that it would be inequitable for the trustee to recover against these defendants. The court stated that defrauded creditors would have their own claims against the same defendants and if the trustee sued for damages, this would deprive the creditors of standing to raise those claims. *Id.* The court's rationale is hard to follow. If the trustee and the creditors have different claims, and if the trustee recovers and makes a distribution to creditors, this does not deprive the creditors of standing to bring their claims. It only reduces their damage claim to the extent they have received a distribution from the estate. *See Drabkin v. L & L Constr. Assoc. (In re Latin Inv. Corp.),* 168 B.R. 1, 6 (Bankr.D.D.C.1993).

Defendants also cite *Begier v. Price Waterhouse,* 81 B.R. 303 (E.D.Pa.1987), but that case does not support defendants' position. There, the court dismissed one count of a complaint brought by a Chapter 11 trustee against the debtor's former accountant. However, the dismissed count asserted claims on behalf of creditors. Two counts of the complaint remained in the case, and these counts involved claims that the defendant accounting firm breached its contract with the debtor and negligently performed the accounting services causing the debtor to suffer financial loss.

The recent case of *Hirsch v. Arthur Andersen & Co.*, 178 B.R. 40 (D.Conn.1994), points out why trustees in Ponzi cases often have trouble pleading claims on behalf of the estate distinct from the claims of defrauded creditors. The difficulty arises in the description and measurement of damages. The court in *Hirsch* stated: "In the standing context, the concept of damage to the debtors is a difficult one to understand, and one that has been applied inconsistently by the courts." *Id.* at 43. In *Hirsch,* the court dismissed the Chapter 11 trustee's claims against certain law firms and accountants that allegedly participated with the debtors in a Ponzi scheme. Like the defendants in the instant case, the defendants in *Hirsch* argued that the trustee lacked standing because the claims "really" belonged to the creditors and that any claims the debtors might assert were barred by virtue of their own participation in the fraudulent scheme. The court found the trustee lacked standing largely because of the way he alleged damages to the debtor. The bulk of the complaint alleged a scheme to defraud creditors and the only damage to the debtor was the extent of the unpaid obligations of the debtors to the creditors. It was fatal that the trustee had not alleged any distinct way in which the debtors were damaged by the asserted wrongdoing of the defendants. The court stated that if the facts of the complaint suggest that the claims actually belong to the creditors, a blanket allegation of damage to the debtors will not confer standing on the trustee.

[3][4] Before discussing cases in which the courts have found standing, it is important to note a fallacy in the argument that the claims asserted "really" belong to the investors/creditors. This argument often comes from the mistaken notion that the creditors are the ones who will receive the money anyway, so why not let them pursue the wrongdoers themselves and do away with the trustee.[FN4] This argument misunderstands the nature of bankruptcy and the role of the trustee in bankruptcy. Bankruptcy is a collective debt collection device. Indeed, the trustee's job is to investigate the debtor's financial affairs, liquidate assets, pursue the debtor's causes of action, and acquire assets through the trustee's avoiding powers in order to make a distribution to creditors. "The concept of a trustee in bankruptcy is that of a creditor representative whose single effort will replace that of

multiple and often wasteful and competitive efforts of individual creditors." 1 Daniel R. Cowans et al., *Cowans Bankruptcy Law and Practice* § 2.7, at 72 (1986 ed.). To find that the trustee has no standing to pursue causes of action belonging to the debtor because the recovery would only benefit the creditors is an absurd argument, given the fact that the trustee's goal is to make a distribution to creditors.

> FN4. This argument seems to have been accepted in *Williams* and *Hirsch*. In *Williams*, the court said that "the investors plainly remain the real parties in interest" in the trustee's suit because the estate will only recoup administrative costs and investor-assignors will receive the bulk of the recovery. *Williams*, 859 F.2d at 666. In *Hirsch*, the court stated that since the trustee alleged that the injury to the debtors was coextensive with the injury to the creditors, "the trustee has done no more than cast the debtors as collection agents for the creditors." *Hirsch*, 178 B.R. at 44.

In cases in which the courts have held the trustee had standing, the courts have read the complaint to allege a claim belonging to the debtor or an injury to the debtor conceptually distinct from the injury to defrauded investors or creditors. In *Regan v. Vinick & Young (In re Rare Coin Galleries of America, Inc.)*, 862 F.2d 896 (1st Cir.1988), the court held that the trustee had standing to bring an action against accountants. The debtor bought, sold, and invested in rare coins for its customers, and the principals misappropriated assets leading the firm into bankruptcy. The trustee sued the accountant and auditor for certifying reports which summarized rare coin transactions. The complaint alleged negligence, breach of contract, negligent misrepresentation, and unfair and deceptive acts or practices. The damages sought included the cost of the accountant's services, the misappropriation of assets by the debtor's principals, certain commissions paid by the debtor, the costs of bankruptcy, and the cost to the estate of an $11.8 million claim by the Federal Trade Commission on behalf of public consumer creditors. Defendants contended that the claims filed by the trustee belonged only to the creditors, but the court examined the complaint and found otherwise. The court stated:

> In each of the four counts set forth in the complaint the trustee alleges damage to the *debtor*. The four counts

(negligence, breach of contract, negligent misrepresentation and the statutory claim for unfair or deceptive practices) all clearly could have been asserted by the debtor, RCG. The trustee steps into the shoes of the debtor for the purposes of asserting or maintaining the debtor's causes of actions, which become property of the estate. The confusion may stem from the trustee's repeated emphasis upon the assertions that the accountant's wrongdoing caused RCG's customers to lose money. This emphasis on the customers' claims appears to result from the $11.8 million claim filed on their behalf against the estate (the largest against the debtor) and from the concern that the estate may be held jointly and severally liable with the accountant in any eventual actions commenced by the customers. *It is clear that, despite the emphasis on the customers' claims, the trustee is asserting claims that belong to the estate.*

Id. at 900-01 (emphasis added) (footnote omitted) (citation omitted).

[5] The recent Seventh Circuit case of *Scholes v. Lehmann,* 56 F.3d 750 (7th Cir.1995), not cited by the parties, is very helpful in analyzing standing. There, a receiver under Illinois law for corporations owned by a Ponzi scheme principal brought fraudulent conveyance actions against a Ponzi scheme investor, the principal's former spouse, and religious organizations that received funds from the corporations in receivership. The court of appeals held that the receiver had standing to assert the fraudulent conveyance claims. The defendants argued that the receiver was not really suing on behalf of the entity in receivership, but was suing on behalf of the investors who had purchased interests in the corporations. Citing *Caplin,* the defendants argued that a receiver does not have standing to sue on behalf of the creditors of the entity in receivership and that, like a trustee in bankruptcy, an equity receiver may sue only to redress injuries to the entity in receivership. The defendants asked: how could the allegedly fraudulent conveyances hurt the instruments through which the Ponzi scheme was operated? Judge Posner provided the following answer:

> The corporations, Douglas's robotic tools, were nevertheless in the eyes of the law separate legal entities with rights and

duties. They received money from unsuspecting, if perhaps greedy and foolish, investors. That money should have been used for the stated purpose of the corporations' sale of interests in the limited partnerships, which was to trade commodities....

The three sets of transfers removed assets from the corporations for an unauthorized purpose and by doing so injured the corporations.

Scholes, 56 F.3d at 754.

Thus, it is the removal of assets that damaged the debtor, and the trustee has standing to sue for this type of injury.

Measuring the injury to the debtor by the money going out (looting, embezzlement, waste, etc.) rather than by the money coming in (funds raised by defrauding investors) was significant in *Drabkin*, 168 B.R. at 1. There, the court found the trustee had standing to assert claims of fraud and conspiracy against defendants who helped the debtor's principals breach duties to the debtor and bring about the demise of the debtor. The court interpreted the claims as claims for fraud against the debtor based on misuse of corporate funds. The court held the trustee alleged a viable cause of action to the extent intentional mismanagement and misuse allowed defendants and the debtor's principals to loot the corporation of its assets. The damages would include "damages from the looting itself as well as damages inflicted in perpetuating the debtor's existence past the point of insolvency in order to loot." *Id.* at 5.

Now we turn to the complaint in this case to determine if the trustee has alleged claims belonging to the debtor and/or injuries to the debtor as opposed to injuries to defrauded investors. The specific claims against the Accountant Defendants are set forth in ¶¶ 76-85 of the Complaint. The particular wrongful acts alleged are that the accounting firm prepared false and materially misleading financial statements from 1987 through 1992; that the accounting firm prepared false tax returns based on these statements; that the accounting firm systematically departed from generally accepted accounting principles in preparing financial statements; that the accounting firm failed to alert the management, board of directors, or other parties of known errors and omissions in the financial statements it compiled; and that the accounting firm negligently concealed Plaza's insolvency from Plaza's board of directors and shareholders from 1989 through 1993. The claims against the Accountant Defendants also incorporate by reference the alleged claims against Basroon. In pertinent part, the trustee alleges that Basroon engaged in acts of self-dealing with Plaza through a corporation known as Barob, Inc., which served to drain funds from Plaza to the detriment of Plaza.

In addition to the separate claims against the Accountant Defendants, the Complaint alleges a set of claims against all defendants for a fraudulent conspiracy.[FN5] (Compl. ¶¶ 86-91.) The allegations are that all the defendants participated in a conspiracy designed to maintain the Ponzi scheme and to promote each defendant's personal financial or business interest. As a result of these activities, Plaza incurred millions of dollars of liabilities to investors which it could not repay.

> FN5. The Complaint also contains general claims against all defendants for fraudulent conveyances. (Compl. ¶¶ 92-94.) This claim states that each defendant has transferred property in order to avoid liabilities to the trustee. The parties have not addressed this claim in the two motions.

The claims as pled certainly look like claims belonging to the debtor rather than creditors. However, the damages alleged are vague. The Complaint simply alleges that Basroon's actions and the accounting firm's actions drove Plaza into bankruptcy and the damages exceed $9 million. In response to an interrogatory, the trustee stated that his overall damage could be calculated by ascertaining the difference between the amount invested in Plaza and the value of the estate on the date the bankruptcy petition was filed. The Accountant Defendants argue that if the trustee's damages equal the total of creditor claims in this case, then the claims belong to the creditors and this adversary proceeding should be dismissed. However, the trustee contends this was a preliminary damage analysis and that other damage analyses may be employed, depending on the particular defendant. He points out that the response to his interrogatory stated that it was not a final statement of damages claimed as to any party and that as to the Accountant Defendants, damages would include the fees paid to the accounting firm.

At this stage of the proceeding, it would be unfair to dismiss the trustee's claims, because he has done a preliminary damage analysis based on the difference between the amount invested and the assets on hand. The allegations in the Complaint suggest that damages would be better calculated by reference to monies improperly used by Basroon, accounting fees paid, and other accepted methods of measuring damages suffered by debtors.

[6] In the form pretrial order used in this district, a plaintiff is required to specify damages. Rather than wait for the preparation of the full Pretrial Order involving many parties, it makes sense at this juncture to have the plaintiff file a Statement of Damages Sought Against the Accountant Defendants. Thus, plaintiff is directed to file a pleading on or before October 10, 1995, containing a separate statement for each item of damage claimed against the Accountant Defendants, and a brief description of the item of damage, the dollar amount claimed, and citation to the law, rule, regulation, or any decision authorizing recovery for that particular item of damage. In specifying damages, counsel should consider the message from the case law that damages to the debtor are best measured by outgoing money rather than by incoming money.

In conclusion, the trustee does have standing to assert the claims against the Accountant Defendants. The claims of malpractice and fraud on the debtor by Basroon as an accountant belong to the debtor. However, the method of measuring damages will need to be refined, and the trustee will be given an opportunity to clarify the elements of the damages claimed.

This result is not inconsistent with *Caplin, Hadley* and *Williams*. The trustees in those cases did not assert that any claim existed on behalf of the debtors, and the court in *E.F. Hutton* emphasized that its holding was restricted to the specific facts of that case. In addition, one of the courts' concerns is duplicative litigation, and the pendency of other lawsuits by creditors has been a factor in the decision to dismiss the trustee's claims. In *E.F. Hutton*, the court found duplicative litigation had already occurred, with aspects of the litigation pending in three separate courts. *E.F. Hutton*, 901 F.2d at 987.

In *Feltman,* the court took judicial notice that a complaint by creditors was pending in state court which duplicated some of the claims in the trustee's suit. *Feltman,* 122 B.R. at 474 n. 11. In *Hirsch,* the investors had already asserted actions against the defendants. *Hirsch,* 178 B.R. at 44. In the case at bar, counsel have not advised the Court of any pending duplicative litigation by creditors against these Accountant Defendants.

[7][8] Before turning to the *in pari delicto* argument, the Court notes there are some lessons to be learned from the standing cases regarding how a trustee in bankruptcy should plead a claim against a third-party participant in a Ponzi scheme in order to survive a motion to dismiss. A trustee should be careful to plead claims belonging to the debtor and injury to the debtor. A trustee should be careful not to plead for a recovery based on any injury to the investors/creditors, even though the fraud on the investors will be a part of the background allegations. In alleging background facts, trustees often explain how investors have been defrauded. These background facts, however, should not be confused with the claims of the trustee. A trustee should be careful not to plead damages as an amount equal to the funds invested in the debtor's Ponzi scheme, but should measure damages based on funds improperly paid out by the debtor.

Finally, the Statute of Limitations Motion appears to be mooted in large part by this ruling. In that Motion, the Accountant Defendants are generally seeking a declaration that the trustee is precluded from asserting as an element of damages any of the funds invested in Plaza prior to April 5, 1989 or any obligations to investors that Plaza incurred prior to April 5, 1989. Based on the above reasoning pertaining to the Standing Motion, damages to the debtor will not be calculated based on funds invested.

II. The *In Pari Delicto* Argument

The other ground for the Accountant Defendants' Standing Motion is the argument that the trustee's claims are barred as a matter of law by the doctrine of *in pari delicto.* This argument raises more difficult factual and legal issues that are not fully developed by the present record.

[9][10][11][12] First, would the doctrine of *in pari delicto* apply to bar the debtor Plaza from suing the Accountant Defendants outside of bankruptcy?

The answer to this question depends on whether the acts and knowledge of Martin Basroon are imputed to the debtor Plaza. The trustee argues that the adverse interest exception applies here and that Basroon's knowledge should not be imputed to the corporation. The Accountant Defendants respond that the sole representative doctrine applies to prevent the trustee from asserting the adverse interest doctrine.[FN6] While the question of whether Basroon's knowledge and actions can be imputed to Plaza is a question of law, the proper application of these doctrines requires a close examination of the facts. The Court cannot determine from the current record which facts pertaining to these legal issues are disputed and which facts are undisputed.

> FN6. The adverse interest exception is an exception to the general rule that a corporation is charged with constructive knowledge of all material facts of which its officers or agents acquire knowledge. Where an officer or agent is engaged in a scheme to defraud a corporation, "the presumption that knowledge held by the agent was disclosed to the [corporation] fails because he cannot be presumed to have disclosed that which would expose and defeat his fraudulent purpose." *CEPA Consulting, Ltd. v. King Main Hurdman (In re Wedtech Corp.)*, 138 B.R. 5, 9 (S.D.N.Y.1992) (quoting *Center v. Hampton Affiliates, Inc.*, 66 N.Y.2d 782, 497 N.Y.S.2d 898, 488 N.E.2d 828, 829 (N.Y.1985)); *see also* 3 William M. Fletcher, *Fletcher Cyclopedia of the Law of Private Corporations* § 819 (perm.ed.1986).

> The "sole representative" or "sole actor" doctrine is an exception to the adverse interest exception. In cases where the business or transaction in question is entrusted to an officer or agent of the corporation as its sole representative, the adverse interest exception does not apply and the knowledge of the officer or agent is imputable to the corporation. The reason for the rule is that, where the officer in question is the sole representative of that corporation, there is no one to whom to impart his knowledge and no one from whom he may conceal it. Fletcher, *supra,* § 827.

The initial Statement of Material Facts presented with the Standing Motion did not address any of the facts pertinent to the applicability of either the adverse interest exception or the sole representative doctrine. Such facts include, but are not limited to, Plaza's ownership and the other shareholders' knowledge, involvement, and acquiescence. Accordingly, the Court has requested counsel to confer and submit a joint statement of which facts relevant to these issues are undisputed and which facts are disputed.

[13] There is also the important question of which state law of imputation applies. State law, not federal law, governs the imputation of knowledge to corporate victims of alleged negligence. *O'Melveny & Myers v. FDIC*, 512 U.S. 79, ----, 114 S.Ct. 2048, 2053, 129 L.Ed.2d 67 (1994). The Court cannot tell from the briefs what the parties contend regarding which state's laws apply. The trustee's brief contains footnotes suggesting that perhaps Florida law or New Jersey law should apply, but there is no discussion of what the law of those states is regarding imputation. In the defendants' reply brief, they take the position that the law of Georgia should apply "to the tort issues," but they state that the issue of which state law applies is academic. In response, the trustee disputes whether the choice of law issue is academic and again mentions that it could be New Jersey, Georgia, or Florida.

Counsel need to determine if there is a choice of law issue to decide, i.e., whether they agree or disagree on which state law governs the *in pari delicto* and imputation of knowledge issues. If counsel agree on which state law applies, they need to submit briefs on the law of that state as it applies to the facts. If counsel disagree on which state law governs, they need to submit briefs on which state law should govern and why and what the law of that state is as it applies to these facts.

Assuming that the debtor's claims would be barred by *in pari delicto* outside of bankruptcy under some applicable state law, the more interesting (and possibly dispositive) question is whether the *in pari delicto* defense applies to the trustee in bankruptcy here. Again, the briefs filed do not address this question adequately. The briefs do not consider the legal principles established by the Supreme Court case of *O'Melveny & Myers v. FDIC* or the pertinent state law.

In *O'Melveny,* the issue was whether, in a suit by the Federal Deposit Insurance Corporation ("FDIC") as receiver of a federally-insured savings and loan ("S & L"), it is a federal-law or state-law rule of decision that governs the tort liability of attorneys who provided services to the S & L. A unanimous Supreme Court concluded that a state-law rule of decision governs.

The FDIC had sued the lawyers for the S & L, alleging professional negligence and breach of fiduciary duty. The defendants argued that knowledge of the conduct of the controlling officers must be imputed to the S & L and hence to the FDIC which, as receiver, stood in the shoes of the S & L. The FDIC contended that even though the causes of action were created under California law, federal common law determined whether knowledge by officers of the S & L would be imputed to the FDIC when it sues as receiver. The Court examined the Financial Institutions Reform, Recovery, and Enforcement Act of 1989 ("FIRREA") and in particular 12 U.S.C. § 1821(d)(2)(A)(i), which provides that the FDIC succeeds to all the rights, title, powers, and privileges of the insured depository institution. The Court stated that in litigation by the FDIC asserting the claims of the S & L, any defense good against the original party is good against the receiver, and that FIRREA did not authorize the creation of any federal common law with respect to the rights of a receiver. The Court also held that even if FIRREA were not applicable, this was not one of those extraordinary cases in which the judicial creation of a federal rule of decision was warranted. The Supreme Court remanded the case to the Ninth Circuit for a determination of whether California law estopped a receiver from making a claim that would not be available to the corporation because the wrongdoers' knowledge was imputed to the corporation.

On remand, the Ninth Circuit considered whether the FDIC had any rights or defenses not available to the entity it replaced as a result of California law. *FDIC v. O'Melveny & Myers*, 61 F.3d 17 (9th Cir.1995). The Ninth Circuit concluded that the FDIC was not barred by certain equitable defenses that the law firm defendants could have raised against the failed S & L. Referring to California case law, the court found there are exceptions to the general rules that a receiver occupies no better position than that which was occupied by the person for whom he acts and that any defense good against the original party is good against the receiver. One exception is that "defenses based on a party's unclean hands or inequitable conduct do not generally apply against that party's receiver." *Id.* at 18-19 (citing *Camerer*

v. California Sav. & Commercial Bank, 4 Cal.2d 159, 48 P.2d 39, 44-45 (1935)).
The Court further stated:

> While a party may itself be denied a right or defense on
> account of its misdeeds, *there is little reason to impose the same
> punishment on a trustee,* receiver or similar innocent entity
> that steps into the party's shoes pursuant to court order or
> operation of law.... As we noted in our earlier opinion:
>
> A receiver, *like a bankruptcy trustee* and unlike a normal
> successor in interest, does not voluntarily step into the
> shoes of the bank; it is thrust into those shoes.

O'Melveny & Myers, 61 F.3d at 18-20 (emphasis added). The Ninth Circuit
concluded that the equities are different when a receiver is involved, such
that equitable defenses good against the wrongdoer should not be available
against the receiver.

Similar reasoning is found in the recent Seventh Circuit case of *Scholes v.
Lehmann,* 56 F.3d at 750, where the court held the defense of *in pari delicto*
could not be used against an Illinois receiver. The court stated: "the defense
of *in pari delicto* loses its sting when the person who was *in pari delicto* is
eliminated." *Id.* at 754. The reason for holding the entity in receivership
bound by the acts of the bad management is gone once the receiver has
been appointed. In vivid language, the court explained:

> The appointment of the receiver removed the wrongdoer
> from the scene. The corporations were no longer
> Douglas's evil zombies. Freed from his spell they became
> entitled to the return of the moneys-for the benefit not of
> Douglas but of innocent investors-that Douglas had made
> the corporations divert to unauthorized purposes.

Id.

Is there any reason why the rationale of the Ninth Circuit in *O'Melveny* on
remand and the Seventh Circuit in *Scholes* shouldn't apply to the trustee

here? A trustee in bankruptcy has a role similar to the FDIC in *O'Melveny* and the Illinois receiver in *Scholes,* and a trustee in bankruptcy should be in no worse position than a state or federal receiver. Indeed, the courts in both those cases analogized their receivers to trustees in bankruptcy. However, in *O'Melveny,* the Court referenced California law and in *Scholes* the court referenced an Illinois case. As we know from the Supreme Court decision in *O'Melveny,* the application of the equitable defense depends on state law. The parties here have not briefed the State law of Georgia, New Jersey, or Florida (whichever may apply) on the critical issue of whether a receiver collecting assets for the benefit of creditors can be held *in pari delicto* as to the wrongful acts of the entity in receivership. It would be imprudent for the Court to decide this issue without briefs from the parties both on the state law and the significance of *O'Melveny* to this case.

The law cited by the defendants on this issue is not helpful. They cite two cases for the general proposition that the trustee is subject to the same defenses as the debtor when it asserts a debtor's cause of action. These cases, however, did not involve *in pari delicto,* questions of imputability, or the invocation of any equitable defense. *Hays & Co. v. Merrill Lynch, Pierce, Fenner & Smith, Inc.,* 885 F.2d 1149 (3rd Cir.1989) (trustee bound by arbitration clause in debtor's prepetition contract); *Boyajian v. DeFusco (In re Giorgio),* 862 F.2d 933 (1st Cir.1988) (trustee bound by a state supreme court judgment that debtors waived usury defense). The Accountant Defendants then cite *E.F. Hutton* and *Williams* for the proposition that the doctrine of *in pari delicto* should bar the trustee's claims, but the discussion of *in pari delicto* in these cases is limited and is only *dicta.* Neither case held that the *in pari delicto* doctrine would apply to bar a trustee from asserting claims. Neither case analyzes the state law issues as required by the Supreme Court in *O'Melveny.* Both cases simply note that in pari delicto *may* exist between the debtor and the wrongdoer so as to allow a claim of subrogation against the estate. Here, the trustee is suing on behalf of the debtor, not creditors, and there is no danger of defendants becoming subrogated to the rights of creditors against the debtor. *See Drabkin,* 168 B.R. at 6. Finally, defendants' reliance on *CEPA Consulting, Ltd. v. Main Hurdman (In re Wedtech Corp.),* 138 B.R. 5 (S.D.N.Y.1992), is also misplaced. This case was decided before *O'Melveny* and the opinion does not address whether imputation defenses were applicable under state law to a receiver.

The Court concludes that the trustee has standing to assert the claims, but the trustee will have an opportunity to refine and clarify the elements of damages. As to the defendants' *in pari delicto* argument, counsel will need to supplement the record and brief additional issues identified above. A briefing schedule will be established by a separate Order.

IT IS SO ORDERED.

Courtesy of Neil C. Gordon, Partner, Arnall Golden Gregory LLP

APPENDIX D

FCA CRIMINAL REFERRAL FORM

Instructions

Purpose

The FCA Criminal Referral Form (hereinafter FCA Referral Form), which is attached, provides Farm Credit System (FCS or System) institutions and FCA examiners with the means to make referrals to law enforcement agencies of known or suspected criminal activity perpetrated against the institution by insiders (i.e., institution personnel, such as directors, officers, employees, agents, or other persons participating in the conduct or affairs of such institution) or others, such as borrowers. The FCA Referral Form should be used in all cases where known or suspected criminal violations of the type described in 12 CFR Part 617 are discovered by an institution or an examiner. For the purposes of this form, "suspected criminal activity" means that there is a reasonable basis to conclude that a crime has occurred or is occurring.

Filing Requirements

In accordance with FCA Regulations at 12 CFR Part 617, the FCA Referral Form should be filed within 30 calendar days of determining that a known or suspected criminal violation meeting the reporting threshold has occurred. This form should be filled out as completely as practicable under the circumstances. Section 1 and only those pertinent sections need to be forwarded to the law enforcement authorities. Comments should be limited to factual statements, and under no circumstances should the preparer express views on the guilt of any suspect(s). When a known or suspected criminal violation requires urgent attention or is ongoing, the institution should immediately notify law enforcement authorities by telephone before filing the FCA Referral Form. Examiners should follow the procedures in EM-640 for filing an FCA Referral Form.

Where to File:

IF THE FCA REFERRAL FORM IS PREPARED BY AN FCS INSTITUTION:

1. Send the original form to the U.S. Attorney for the region in which the acts took place.

2. Retain one copy of the form, along with the supporting document(s), for 10 years. (Generally, the statute of limitations for most financial banking crimes is 10 years.) Institutions do not need to forward copies of supporting documents.

3. Send one complete copy of the FCA Referral Form to the following offices as appropriate:

   a. If the System institution is a Farm Credit Bank or a Federal Land Bank Association, the Referral Form must be sent to:

      1. The U.S. Secret Service and,
      2. If the known or suspected criminal violation involves the Federal money laundering statutes, the Federal Bureau of Investigation.

   b. All other System institutions must forward the Referral Form to:

      1. The Federal Bureau of Investigation and,
      2. If the known or suspected criminal violation involves either the Federal money laundering or computer fraud statutes, the U.S. Secret Service.

   c. If a System institution cannot determine the appropriate Federal law enforcement investigatory agency to forward the Referral Form to or if there appears to be overlapping jurisdiction to investigate the violations noted in the Referral Form, the System institution should forward the Referral Form to both the Federal Bureau of Investigation and the U.S. Secret Service.

d. U.S. Customs Service for the region in which the acts took place if wire fraud is known or suspected.

e. Internal Revenue Service for the region in which the acts took place if any tax or money laundering/structuring violations are known or suspected.

f. U.S. Postal Service for the region in which the acts took place if mail fraud is known or suspected.

4. Send one complete copy of the FCA Referral Form to:

Office of General Counsel
Farm Credit Administration
1501 Farm Credit Drive
McLean, VA 22102-5090
(703) 883-4020

5. Send one complete copy of the FCA Referral Form to other appropriate Federal, State, or local prosecuting or regulatory agencies if the suspected acts violate other Federal, State, or local law.

IF THE FCA REFERRAL FORM IS PREPARED BY AN FCA EXAMINER/EMPLOYEE:

1. Send the original form to the FCA's Office of General Counsel.
2. Retain one copy in the workpapers.
3. Send one copy to the FCS institution's Board of Directors, as appropriate.

Form

Date: _____

Section I - BACKGROUND INFORMATION

1. Name, location, and phone number of the FCS institution:

   Name:

   Location:

   Street

   City   State   Zip Code

   Phone number:

If transaction occurred at branch office(s), please specify the branch name and address:

2. Asset size of institution: $_____

3. Approximate date and dollar amount involved in suspected violation(s):

   Date: _____   Amount: _____

4. The following violation of the criminal code of the United States may have occurred:

   ☐ Conversion[1]   (18 U.S.C. 658)   Complete Section II
   ☐ False Statement[a] (18 U.S.C. 1014) Complete Section III
   ☐ False Entry, etc.[a](18 U.S.C. 1006) Complete Section IV
   ☐ Misappropriation, etc.[a] (18 U.S.C. 657) Complete Section V
   ☐ Other[2] (18 U.S.C. _____)Complete Section VI

---

[1] Excerpt of the statute in EM-640 of the *FCA Examination Manual*.

[2] See, e.g., 18 U.S.C. §§ 212, 213, 215, 216, 371, 493, 709, 1011, 1013, 1907, and 1909.

5. This matter is being referred to the U.S. Attorney in:

    City   State   Judicial District (if known)

    and, as applicable, to the FBI in:

    City   State

    and/or the U.S. Secret Service in

    City   State

    Other:

6. Person(s) suspected of criminal violation (if more than one, use a continuation sheet):

    a. Name:
                       First   M.I.   Last
        Address:

                  Street   City   State   Zip Code

        Date of birth (if known):

        Social Security number (if known):

    b. Identity of suspect (check all appropriate boxes):

        Insider

        ☐   Officer   ☐ Borrower   ☐ Other (specify) ____
        ☐   Employee   ☐ Unknown suspect
        ☐   Director
        ☐   Agent

c. If the suspect is an insider, is the person currently affiliated with the institution?

☐ Yes ☐ No

If no, ☐ terminated ☐ resigned ☐ other (specify)

Date:

Describe circumstances of separation as appropriate (if necessary, use a continuation sheet):

d. Prior or related referrals of this individual?

☐ Yes ☐ No

If yes, please describe the basis for the prior referral:

e. Referral pertaining to another individual arising out of or related to this referral?

☐ Yes ☐ No

If yes, please describe the basis for this related referral:

f. Is person affiliated with any other financial institution?

☐ Yes ☐ No

Is person affiliated with any other business enterprise?

☐ Yes ☐ No

If yes to either or both, please identify:

7. Offer of assistance:

The individuals listed below are/will be authorized to discuss this referral with appropriate law enforcement officials and to assist in locating or explaining any document pertinent to this referral:

Name   Phone No.
Name   Phone No.
Name   Phone No.

8. FCA Referral Form prepared by:

Position: FCA Examiner? ☐ Yes ☐ No

Institution (if other than the FCS institution previously identified):

Phone No.

Address:

Date:

THE FOLLOWING SECTIONS OF THE REFERRAL ARE CRITICAL. They should be as detailed as circumstances permit. The care with which this section is written may make the difference in whether or not the described conduct and its criminal nature are clearly understood. The discussion points listed in these sections are not exhaustive. Feel free to use attachments or to continue the description on a separate sheet. Include any suggestions for interviewing witnesses, gathering documents, or anything else which might prove useful.

Section II - CONVERSION

(18 U.S.C. 658)

1. Note(s):

   Date
   Amount
   Maturity
   Balance due as of this date

2. Identity of the security instrument:

   ☐ Financing statement/security agreement
   ☐ Chattel mortgage
   ☐ Other
   Office of filing
   Date filed

3. Information about property converted:

   a. Type of property

☐ Livestock:	kind	breed	number
	brands		
	other identifying data		
☐ Equipment:	type	model	year
	serial number		
	other identifying data		
☐ Crops: kind	quantity		
☐ Other			

   b. Value at date of conversion
   c. Valuation basis
   d. Usual location of property if different from address of borrower shown in Section I
   e. The property was disposed of by the borrower on or about:

by sale ☐   pledge ☐   other ☐
(explain)   to

Street   City   County State

for the sum of $_____.

4. The conversion resulted in a loss (or potential loss) to the System institution identified in Section I in the amount of $_____.

5. Witnesses (names, addresses, and brief description of expected testimony):

6. Other persons suspected of criminal violation (names, addresses, and brief description of involvement):

7. Present whereabouts of borrower if different from address shown in Section I:

8. Did borrower request consent to dispose of any of the collateral?

   ☐ Yes   ☐ No

   Has borrower applied proceeds of the conversion to the loan secured by the collateral?

   ☐ Yes   ☐ No   ☐ In part

9. Had borrower previously disposed of collateral without consent?

   ☐ Yes   ☐ No

   Did borrower previously apply proceeds of the conversion to the loan secured by the collateral?

   ☐ Yes   ☐ No   ☐ In part

10. Is disposition of collateral by debtors without the consent of creditors a customary practice in the community?

☐ Yes   ☐ No

11. If this matter has been reported to local authorities, state when and to whom the report was made and any action taken:

12. Describe any civil action taken or to be taken to prevent or recover loss:

Section III - FALSE STATEMENT

(18 U.S.C. 1014)

1. Available information indicates that a false statement regarding assets, liabilities, or other information was made on:

   ☐   loan application
   ☐   other documents   Identify:

2. The document containing the false statement was prepared by

3. Statement was false because (explain)

4. The statement was relied on by the FCS institution identified in Section I, which took the following action as a result: made a loan in the amount of $ or other (explain)

5. The action described in item 4 resulted in a loss (or potential loss) to the System institution in the amount of $

6. Witnesses (names, addresses, and brief description of expected testimony):

7. Other persons suspected of criminal violation (names, addresses, and brief description of involvement):

8. Present whereabouts of person named in Section I if different from the address shown in that section:

9. If this matter has been reported to local authorities, state when and to whom the report was made and any action taken:

10. Describe any civil action taken or to be taken to prevent or recover loss:

Section IV - FALSE ENTRY, ETC.

(18 U.S.C. 1006)

1. Available information indicates that the person named in Section I:

    ☐ made a false entry in a book, report, or statement to the System institution identified in Section I. (Describe the nature of the false entry.)

    ☐ without being authorized, drew an order or bill of exchange, made an acceptance, or issued, put forth, or assigned a note, debenture, bond, or other obligation, or draft, bill of exchange, mortgage, judgment, or decree.

    Identity of the document:

    ☐ participated or shared in or received directly or indirectly money, profit, property, or benefits through a transaction, loan, commission, contract, or other act of the System institution.

    Description of what was received and the type of transaction:

2. The action described in item 1 resulted in a loss (or potential loss) to the System institution in the amount of $

3. Witnesses (names, addresses, and brief description of expected testimony):

4. Other persons suspected of criminal violation (names, addresses, and brief description of involvement):

5. Present whereabouts of person named in Section I if different from the address shown in that section:

6. If this matter has been reported to local authorities, state when and to whom the report was made and any action taken:

7. Describe any civil action taken or to be taken to prevent or recover loss:

Section V - MISAPPROPRIATION, ETC.

(18 U.S.C. 657)

1. Kind of property misappropriated (money, securities, or other things of value belonging to the System institution identified in Section I):

2. Value of property misappropriated (embezzled, abstracted, purloined, willfully misapplied): $

3. Disposition of property misappropriated:

4. Witnesses (names, addresses, and brief description of expected testimony):

5. Other person(s) suspected of criminal violation (names, addresses, and brief description of involvement):

6. Present whereabouts of person named in Section I if different from the address shown in that section:

7. If this matter has been reported to local authorities, state when and to whom the report was made and the action taken:

8. Describe any civil action taken or to be taken to prevent or recover loss:

Section VI - OTHER

Describe the offense, when it occurred and the cost to the System institution, if any. Provide the names and addresses of witnesses and a brief description of their expected testimony. State the present whereabouts of the person(s) named in Section I if different from the address shown in that section. Attach a narrative report describing any other pertinent statements and documents.

Courtesy of Stephanie E. Kaiser, Partner, McGinnis, Lochridge & Kilgore LLP

APPENDIX E

SAMPLE PETITION

CAUSE NO. 1234567

JOHN Q. PUBLIC,	§	IN THE
Plaintiff,	§	DISTRICT COURT
	§	
v.	§	1ST JUDICIAL DISTRICT
	§	
WHEELER DEALER,	§	
ANY BANK, and	§	
MAYBERRY COFFEE	§	
IMPORTS, INC.,	§	
Defendants.	§	SOME COUNTY, TEXAS

PLAINTIFF'S AMENDED PETITION

TO THE HONORABLE JUDGE:

Plaintiff John Q. Public ("Plaintiff") files this Amended Petition and in support of same would respectfully show the Court as follows:

I.
Discovery Designation

1.   Plaintiff intends that discovery be conducted under a Level 3 Discovery Plan pursuant to the scheduling order in place.

II.
Parties

2.   Plaintiff is a natural person and a resident of Some County, Texas.

3.   Defendant Any Bank (the "Bank") is a bank authorized to do business in Texas and has appeared in this cause for all purposes.

4.   Defendant Wheeler Dealer ("Wheeler") is an individual residing in Texas and who has appeared in this cause for all purposes.

5.   Defendant Mayberry Coffee Imports, Inc. ("MI") is a Texas corporation and has appeared in this cause for all purposes.

III.
Jurisdiction and Venue

6.   Jurisdiction and venue are proper in the district court of Some County, Texas. Plaintiff's injuries and damages occurred therein and Defendants conducted business in Some County, Texas. Plaintiff has been damaged in an amount within the jurisdictional limits of this Court.

IV.
Factual Background

7.   This case involves shocking and outrageous conduct by the Bank, who knowingly and intentionally assisted, facilitated, and permitted the check kite scheme to unfold, involving approximately $100 million in money floating in and out of one account at the Bank in 2001 and 2002 alone. This fraudulent scheme involved the Bank aiding, abetting, and inducing its accountholder, MI, and its principal, Wheeler, to deposit checks every day to cover checks that were not drawn on collected funds in order to perpetuate a multi-year bank fraud. Despite the Bank's legal obligations to prevent this conduct and to report this type of Suspected Activity, the Bank knowingly allowed the kite to continue to grow for years, profiting by charging staggering amounts of fees on the serial overdrafting.

8.   Since before 1999, Wheeler wholly owned and managed MI, an imported coffee shop, and owned a retail store, ABCD Retail ("ABCD"), with locations in Mayberry and Mount Pilot. In 2000, Wheeler formed ABCD as majority shareholder with Plaintiff as the minority shareholder. Wheeler and MI each had a bank account at the Bank. At relevant times: (a) the Bank had accounts of MI, ABCD, and Wheeler; (b) Last State Bank ("Last Bank") had at least two Wheeler accounts; (c) Second State Bank had accounts for MI and ABCD; and (d) Loneliest Star Bank had accounts for MI and ABCD, and possibly a personal account for Wheeler.

9.   No later than 2000, Wheeler had a history of frequently and problematically overdrawing on one or more accounts at the Bank, in particular the account of MI, which resulted in substantial fees and other benefits for the bank but kept Wheeler and MI in a cycle of scrambling to cover overdrafts with money moved into the MI account and then quickly out of the account back to the accounts of other entities. As early as 1997, the Bank expressly allowed Wheeler to overdraw the MI account up to $100,000.00.   Approximately one year later, the Bank increased the overdraft line of credit to $300,000.00. And, in or around 2000, the Bank loaned Wheeler $100,000.00 to pay off his overdrafts (which exceeded $100,000.00 at the time) and then agreed that he could overdraw on the MI account every day *without limitation as to amount* as long as the total amount of checks he brought in totaled more than the overdrafts for that day. By this time, the Bank already knew that: (a) there were substantial overdrafts on the account that had remained unpaid; (b) Wheeler's financial information was opaque; and (c) Wheeler entities' loans were undercapitalized and the business was weak.

10.   In 2000, Wheeler formed ABCD, in which Wheeler was the President and majority shareholder and in which Plaintiff was a minority shareholder.   Wheeler owned 75% of the stock in ABCD and, unlike Plaintiff, who owned 25%, Wheeler was the signatory on its bank accounts and responsible for its daily operations. Plaintiff was neither an employee nor manager of the company.

11.   From at least 1997 through early 2001, the Bank permitted MI to overdraw on its account without limit and paid checks drawn on that account every day in excess of collected funds as long as MI deposited enough checks every day to cover the negative ledger balance (but not the collected or all available balances). The Bank knew the checks came largely from Wheeler-related entities' accounts at other banks and not from legitimate MI business activities.   The Bank also knew the activity in the account was disproportionate to the revenue of the businesses involved. The Bank would inform Wheeler or MI of the amounts required each day by telephone or through online banking. Despite the deposits, the available balance would remain overdrawn every day. This arrangement, which the Bank incorrectly characterizes as an "intra-day overdraft," is in the

regulatory arena known as a check kite. The Bank knew of this kite and this system for years.

12.   Checks written on the ABCD and/or other accounts were deposited into the MI account, having all of the telltale signs of a classic check kiting scheme: (a) the checks had common signators; (b) were made in large, even amounts;   (c) were sequentially numbered; (d) had similar names and (e) were disproportionate to business activities. Despite the suspected kite notifications, the Bank continued to allow Wheeler to overdraw on the account and would pay the checks drawn in excess of collected funds each day.   Neither the Bank nor Wheeler ever notified Plaintiff that checks drawn on the ABCD account were used to "cover" the daily overdrafts at the Bank.

13.   As the Bank knew, its banking arrangement with Wheeler demonstrated the hallmarks of a check kite. Basic indications of a check kite include: use of uncollected funds; account activity that is out of proportion to the customer's business; regular deposits increasing in amounts; deposits and withdrawals in large round numbers; frequent inquiries about account balances; similar signators; checks written to and from the same entities or entities with similar names or ownership; and service charges on the involved accounts often increased due to kiting activity.

14.   The Bank was aware of each check drawn on the MI account: it had personnel trained to confirm where checks came from and to; and the account officer and branch manager, Jane Doe, individually approved each item that would result in an overdraft on the MI account every day. The Bank has admitted it was also aware of Wheeler's deposits and their size every day. The checks and deposits involved in the kite were numerous, came in large, even amounts, and usually brought the negative balance at the end of the day to a point similar to but larger than the negative balance at the start of the day.

15.   In or around 1999, the Bank paid a substantial amount of money to install a new fraud detection software from a company, whose function, in part, was to detect check kites at the bank like ones that the Bank previously had at the bank. The fraud detection software quickly notified

the Bank of the kite in the MI account, and the Bank's fraud department informed account officer, Jane Doe, on multiple occasions that the MI account was suspicious (i.e., a check kite was going on). Ms. Doe instructed the fraud department that she was aware of, and comfortable with, the activity; the fraud department was then permitted to disable (or suspend) the kiting software's ability to send alerts on this particular account for a period of weeks; after the expiration of which, the account would appear on another suspect kiting activity report and would send an alarm to the fraud department of the suspicious activity so that it could be researched and investigated. Notwithstanding the Bank's masking of the kite notifications, at least two bank employees *actually knew* about the kite.

16.   By 2000, the Bank's fraud department, internal auditors, and BSA officer (who is responsible for filing legally-mandated Suspicious Activity Reports) all knew about the existence of the kite, but – with full knowledge and instruction from Ms. Doe – the Bank continued to facilitate the kite and help Wheeler perpetrate the fraud.

17.   In November of 2000, the Bank decided to represent to Wheeler that the kite would be continued for 90 more days and then shut down; it ultimately gave Wheeler the date of February 1, 2001. However, after calculating its exposure on the MI account in terms of number of days, the Bank stopped the kite three days early to maximize incoming receipts and avoid any payment obligation to Last Bank or others. By January 31, 2001, the Bank had created a positive balance in the MI account of $1,000,000.00 (from a prior overdrawn amount of -$900,000.00) by depositing incoming checks and rejecting outgoing checks. As a result, ABCD's accounts at Last Bank were overdrawn. Last Bank looked to Plaintiff and his personal guaranty to cover the entire amount. The Bank used the approximately $2,000,000.00 in deposits from the Last Bank account and other accounts and approximately $200,000.00 in a ABCD account to pay off outstanding loans to MI in which Plaintiff had no interest. As a result, the two businesses in which Plaintiff had invested were destroyed. No employee, officer, or other person at the Bank was ever reprimanded for anything related to the kite and bank fraud at issue in this lawsuit. The Bank has stood by those employees and has ratified the acts of its employees and agents.

18.   Each of these acts directly took monies from businesses in which Plaintiff had an interest for the direct personal benefit of Wheeler and/or companies in which Plaintiff did not have an interest, causing harm to Plaintiff, Plaintiff's business interests, and the businesses in which Plaintiff invested. Plaintiff was never advised nor had knowledge of: (a) the kite; (b) the status of the accounts; or (c) the illegitimate use of trust proceeds to pay the overdrafts at, and/or other amounts allegedly owed to, the Bank. In short, with the Bank's help and guidance, Wheeler improperly used funds from the ABCD accounts for his own personal benefit and/or for the benefit of MI and the Bank at Plaintiff's expense without the prior approval or consent of Plaintiff.

V.
Causes of Action

Count 1 – Breach of Fiduciary Duty and Aiding and Abetting/Conspiracy in a Breach of Fiduciary Duty

19.   Wheeler was a majority shareholder and a 74.25% limited partner in the entities at issue; Plaintiff, by contrast, was a minority shareholder and a 24.75% limited partner in the entities at issue. Wheeler owed Plaintiff a fiduciary duty in dealings relating to the scope of the car dealerships' operations and the businesses at issue in this lawsuit.

20.   Wheeler induced Plaintiff to participate in the companies by investing substantial sums of cash, executing personal guarantees for additional sums of money, and pledging all ownership shares and interests for ABCD's bank loans. Plaintiff invested monies and guaranteed certain loans. As a minority shareholder and limited partner and member, Plaintiff entrusted the day-to-day operations of the entities at issue to Wheeler.

21.   Wheeler abused those confidences by ignoring corporate structures, separate accounting practices, self-dealing prohibitions, and ordinarily prudent management practices. Wheeler granted in himself the unfettered right to repeatedly write/sign/authorize checks on accounts owned the entities at issue for personal expenses, MI expenses or losses, and/or other unauthorized purposes. He used his position and the authority afforded to him to perpetrate the kite at the Bank for years. At all

times, Wheeler's practices were kept from Plaintiff until after the Bank: (a) chose to shut down the kite it had operated through its bank; and (b) set up its plan to cram the kite onto other accounts in order to collect its fees and other amounts, thereby exposing Plaintiff to serious economic damages.

22. Wheeler's actions in running a kite and mismanaging the entities without Plaintiff's knowledge constitute a breach of fiduciary duties.

23. The Bank actively and with knowledge of Wheeler's numerous insufficient transactions at the bank aided and abetted these breaches of fiduciary duties to Plaintiff. the Bank's own witnesses acknowledge an undeniable truth – without the facilitation of instant credit and allowing Wheeler to chronically overdraw accounts and use uncollected funds, the kite scheme never could have happened, and it certainly could not have grown to nearly $200 million by the time the Bank decided to shut it down, push the deficits onto Last Bank, and thereby leave Plaintiff holding the bag.

24. At all times material hereto, the Bank knowingly aided, abetted, participated, substantially encouraged and assisted and conspired with Wheeler to commit tortious acts pursuant to a common design in breach of fiduciary duty. As a result, the Bank is liable to Plaintiff.

25. As a proximate cause of the breach of fiduciary duty and the Bank's aiding and abetting in Wheeler's felony and fraudulent scheme, Plaintiff has suffered millions of dollars in economic and financial injury as discussed above, and seeks all appropriate damages or remedies.

Count 2 – Fraud Counts and Conspiracy to Defraud

26. At all times material hereto, the Bank aided, abetted, assisted, encouraged, instructed, and/or participated in the check kiting scheme with the intent to: (a) defraud and unlawfully appropriate and convert funds from ABCD to MI and the Bank; and (b) permanently deprive Plaintiff of such funds.

27. During the relevant period of time, accounts at the Bank were used by Defendants to execute the check kiting scheme. Defendants' wrongful

actions (i.e., the inducement, assistance, encouragement, instruction, and/or participation in the check kiting scheme and subsequent misappropriation and conversion of the funds of ABCD or MI's and the Bank's use and benefit) constituted fraud and conspiracy to defraud at Texas common law. The Bank, as a conspirator in the fraud, had knowledge of the fraudulent acts and benefited therefrom, agreed, cooperated with, and instructed Wheeler on the course of action of continuing the kite, committed several acts in furtherance of the conspiracy, and therefore is liable, along with the other Defendants, for all damages proximately caused to Plaintiff.

28.   The Bank and MI also concealed the existence of, and their involvement in, the check kiting scheme with the intent to defraud Plaintiff, and permanently deprive Plaintiff of money in excess of the minimum jurisdictional limits of this Court. Plaintiff was not aware of, nor through the exercise of due diligence could have become aware of, Defendants unlawful actions prior to incurring these losses. Wheeler failed to disclose the fraudulent scheme despite a duty to disclose to Plaintiff. Wheeler failed to disclose to Plaintiff and concealed from Plaintiff the facts pertaining to the check kiting scheme and the comingling of funds. The facts were material, and Wheeler knew Plaintiff was unaware of the facts and did not have an equal opportunity to discover the facts. Wheeler was deliberately silent when he had a duty to speak. By failing to disclose the facts, Wheeler intended to induce Plaintiff to refrain from discovering and acting to prevent and terminate the check kiting scheme and the comingling of funds. Plaintiff relied on Wheeler's nondisclosure and was injured as a result of acting without knowledge of the undisclosed facts. Therefore, Defendants' unlawful actions also constitute fraud and have caused serious economic damages to Plaintiff.

Count 3 – Money Had and Received, Misappropriation of Funds, and Unjust Enrichment

29.   As a result of the fraudulent, illegal, and inequitable conduct described above, Defendants have obtained money that in good conscience and in equity they should not have received, which in equity and good conscience belongs to Plaintiff, and thus a cause of action for money had and received is appropriate in favor of Plaintiff to prevent Defendants' unjust enrichment. The Bank does not have a right to retain funds it

obtained by creating, perpetuating, and charging fees for an ever-increasing check kite. Despite the absence of collected funds in the Bank MI account, the Bank essentially created a ledger-balance reflecting funds sufficient to pay its own fees by increasing the deficit in the account by the amount of those fees and having MI "pay" the increase with checks from other banks. When the Bank terminated the kite, it converted the ledger funds created on the books into real money by depositing incoming checks and rejecting all outgoing checks. Thus, only by taking money from other accounts and leaving Last Bank and others with worthless checks did the Bank actually realize its fees. And, because the majority of the amounts the Bank received at the end of the kite came from the account at Last Bank, Last Bank looked to Plaintiff's guaranty to hold him liable for Defendants' fraud and other bad acts. The Bank cannot retain the monies that it siphoned from others, having forced Plaintiff to suffer the damages by trying to replace the money taken from other accounts with his own funds, loans, and loss of his interest in the company. Allowing the Bank to do so would constitute misappropriation of funds and unjustly enrich it at Plaintiff's expense.

30.   The unlawful actions of Defendants as described above have caused damages to Plaintiff in an amount in excess of the minimum jurisdictional limits of this Court.

Count 4 – Negligence and Gross Negligence

31.   The Bank acted negligently and grossly negligent in the performance of its business and banking operations by failing to act as a reasonably prudent entity in the performance of its business and banking operations, including its negligent failure to supervise its employees who knowingly allowed Wheeler to run the kite using the Bank's accounts. In stark violation of reasonable banking standards, applicable law, regulations, and its own policies and procedures, the Bank ignored all the signs of a check kite. The Bank knew about the kiting activity. It received additional indications, software alerts, and notifications concerning the kite by and through its own fraud personnel for years. It admits that it discussed the kite with Wheeler on many occasions. It evaluated the file for suspicions of kiting and for purposes of filing

mandatory reports. Even though the Bank had a superior knowledge of the risk and a right to control this activity, it knowingly, intentionally, recklessly, maliciously, negligently, and with gross negligence aided, participated in, encouraged, facilitated, and assisted Wheeler and MI in creating and continuing this bank fraud. It orchestrated and perpetuated the bank fraud for years and years but continued accruing and assessing fees for itself due to the chronic use of uncollected funds and overdrafts. It is undeniable that the bank fraud at issue could not have persisted in the manner it did without the knowing assistance of the Bank. When the Bank finally set a deadline to shut the kite down, it *actually instructed* Wheeler and MI *in writing* on how to continue kiting for at least two more months before the opportunity would be foreclosed.

32. Not only did the Bank not behave as a reasonably prudent bank, no person involved in this case has ever seen a bank behave in this fashion when faced with a check kite, nor has anyone, including the Bank, encountered a check kite of this magnitude and duration. As a proximate result of Defendants' negligence and gross negligence, Plaintiff has suffered serious economic injury and has been damaged in an amount within the jurisdictional limits of this Court.

VI.
Joint and Several Liability

33. Defendants are jointly and severally liable for the acts or omissions of the other Defendants and any designated responsible third parties as provided for by Texas law, including without limitation, Tex. Civ. Prac. & Rem. Code § 33.013(b)(1) and (b)(2)(J), including Texas Penal Code § 32.45.

34. Additionally, the Bank has authorized and/or ratified the acts of its employees and agents in their course and scope of employment in participating in the check kite and fraud by continuing the check kite and fraud, by refraining from disciplining any of them on account of the kite, and, in fact, granting bonuses to the employees who perpetuated (and perpetrated) the fraud, rewarding them for bringing in the additional fees generated by the check kite.

VII.
Damages and Remedies

35.   As a direct and proximate result of the above, Plaintiff has suffered significant losses in the past and will continue to sustain losses in the future. Plaintiff also seeks a complete disgorgement of all ill-gotten gains by all of the Defendants from their breaching fiduciary duties and aiding, abetting and/or conspiring in those breaches of fiduciary duties including the fees collected by the Bank.

36.   Plaintiff also seeks pre-judgment and post-judgment interest at the maximum rate allowed under Texas law; costs; and attorney's fees under Tex. Civ. Prac. & Rem. Code Ch. 38. *See also* Tex. R. Civ. P. 131.

37.   Plaintiff estimates that his damages exceed two million dollars ($2,000,000) and continue to accrue daily.

VIII.
Punitive Damages

38.   The unlawful conduct of Defendants was committed knowingly, intentionally, recklessly, maliciously, and/or as a result of gross negligence and involved criminal conduct in violation of the banking laws and contrary to Texas Penal Code §32.45. Defendants knowingly, intentionally, recklessly, maliciously, and/or as a result of gross negligence misapplied property they held as a fiduciary or property of a financial institution in a manner that they knew involved substantial risk of loss. In addition to misapplying property (e.g., monies in the accounts at issue), Defendants have conceded under oath that they received and misapplied and used monies and/or proceeds that were to be held in trust. Defendants conceded that they applied such monies to pay off the overdrafts, loans, and other amounts associated with businesses unrelated to ABCD and/or Plaintiff.

39.   Defendants willfully, intentionally, knowingly, recklessly, and maliciously violated the criminal law as well as fiduciary duties, banking regulations, and reasonable standards of business and banking behavior. Accordingly, exemplary damages should be assessed against these Defendants.

40.   Specifically, Defendants acted intentionally, knowingly, recklessly, maliciously, willfully, wantonly, and/or in a grossly negligent manner. TEX. CIV. PRAC. & REM. CODE §§41.003, 41.005, & 41.008(1). Defendants engaged in a check kiting and fraudulent scheme that constitutes a malicious breach of the fiduciary duties owed to Plaintiff. The Bank aided and abetted in these breaches and engaged in acts through its employees and agents in a managerial capacity acting within the course and scope of employment and the Bank has ratified, authorized, and/or approved of the conduct and acts of such employees and agents.

41.   Defendants' conduct, when viewed objectively from their respective standpoint, involved an extreme degree of risk, considering the probability and magnitude of the potential harm to others, namely Plaintiff, and of which Defendants had actual subjective awareness of the risk involved, but nevertheless proceeded with conscious indifference to the rights, safety, or welfare of others. Defendants' actions and inactions demonstrate a conscious disregard for the well being of others and no regard for safe business practices. Such conduct must be punished and deterred. Because the purpose of punitive damages is to punish wrongful conduct and deter future similar conduct, punitive and/or exemplary damages should be assessed against Defendants. In addition, Plaintiff contends that the exemplary damages sought by Plaintiff are not subject to any limitation pursuant to TEX. CIV. PRAC. & REM. CODE §41.008(c)(10) and TEX. CIV. PRAC. & REM. CODE §41.005.

IX.
Conditions Precedent

42.   All conditions precedent have been performed, waived, or have occurred.

X.
Spoliation

43.   In connection with pretrial discovery in this case, the Bank has intentionally destroyed, shredded, or withheld evidence that is relevant to this case. Therefore, Plaintiff asks the Court to submit to the fact-finder an appropriate instruction that the fact-finder presume that the destroyed,

shredded, discarded, intentionally lost, or withheld evidence, including the e-mails and files sent from and stored on the Bank's servers, research and other files created and submitted to management and officer(s) to track, document, and warn of the kite, for instance those transmitted to the account officer in charge, and other documents withheld or destroyed were all unfavorable to the Bank on the issues of the Bank's liability in this case. *Roytberg v. Wal-Mart Stores, Inc.*, 111 S.W.3d 843, 844 (Tex.App.—Dallas 2003, no pet.); *Watson v. Brazos Elec. Coop, Inc.*, 918 S.W.2d 639, 643 (Tex. App.—Waco 1996, writ denied).

XI.
Piercing the Corporate Veil/Alter Ego

44.   Wheeler, through his status and power as majority shareholder and president of ABCD, used that corporation as a sham to perpetrate a fraud on Plaintiff. Wheeler ran ABCD as his alter-ego. Wheeler organized and operated the corporation as a mere tool or business conduit of himself and for his personal benefit. Wheeler, through his shareholder and officer status, established such a unity between himself and the corporation that the separateness of the corporation had ceased, and the failure to hold Wheeler liable for the corporation's conduct that he instigated and caused would result in injustice to Plaintiff. In addition, Wheeler improperly used the corporation to evade legal obligations, including fiduciary duties, owed to Plaintiff, and to hide criminal conduct. Wheeler also comingled assets and integrated the resources of ABCD with those of other entities in which he had ownership interests and which he controlled and operated to achieve a common business purpose and to coordinate and sustain a multi-year fraudulent check kite.

45.   Wheeler, through his status and power as majority owner and manager of the entities at issue, used the entities as a sham to perpetrate a fraud on Plaintiff. Wheeler ran the entity as his alter-ego. Wheeler organized and operated the corporation as a mere tool or business conduit of himself and for his personal benefit. Wheeler, through his majority ownership and managerial status, established such a unity between himself and the corporation that the separateness of the corporation had ceased, and the failure to hold Wheeler liable for the corporation's conduct that he instigated and caused would result in injustice to Plaintiff. In addition,

Wheeler improperly used the corporation to evade legal obligations, including fiduciary duties, owed to Plaintiff, and to hide criminal conduct. Wheeler also comingled assets and integrated the resources of the entity with those of other entities in which he had ownership interests and which he controlled and operated to achieve a common business purpose and to coordinate and sustain a multi-year fraudulent check kite.

46.   Wheeler through his status and power as owner of MI, used that corporation as a sham to perpetrate a fraud on Plaintiff. Wheeler ran MI as his alter-ego. Wheeler organized and operated the corporation as a mere tool or business conduit of himself and for his personal benefit. Wheeler, through his shareholder and officer status, established such a unity between himself and the corporation that the separateness of the corporation had ceased, and the failure to hold Wheeler liable for the corporation's conduct that he instigated and caused would result in injustice to Plaintiff. In addition, Wheeler improperly used the corporation to evade legal obligations, including fiduciary duties, owed to Plaintiff, and to hide criminal conduct. Wheeler also comingled assets and integrated the resources of MI with those of other entities in which he had ownership interests and which he controlled and operated to achieve a common business purpose and to coordinate and sustain a multi-year fraudulent check kite.

XII.
Jury Demand

47.   Plaintiff has demanded a jury trial and has tendered the appropriate fee.

XIII.
Response to Defendant's Special Exceptions
Demanding Maximum Amount

48.   Plaintiff believes that a jury and the Court should decide the appropriate amount of damages that will properly compensate him for Defendants' wrongful conduct at issue in this case. Nevertheless, in response to the Bank's Special Exceptions, and as required by Texas law, Plaintiff seeks an amount to be awarded in the jury's discretion not to

exceed Five Million Dollars ($5,000,000.00) for the actual damages he has sustained, or in reasonable probability in the future will sustain, by Defendants' conduct at issue in this lawsuit. Additionally, Plaintiff seeks punitive damages as allowed by Texas law to punish Defendants for their wrongful conduct. Again, Plaintiff believes that a jury and the Court should decide the appropriate amount of exemplary damages that will properly sere to punis-h and deter similar wrongdoing n the future as the law provides for. Nevertheless, in response to the Bank's Special Exceptions, and as required by Texas law, Plaintiff pleads that an exemplary award should be in an amount to be awarded in the jury's discretion not to exceed the greater of (a) Fifteen Million Dollars ($15,000,000.00) or (b) twenty percent (20%) of the entire, true net worth and assets of each and every one of the Defendants. Plaintiff reserves all rights to replead in accordance with the Texas Rules of Civil Procedure, as the discovery of further evidence may warrant, or in accordance with any Court orders or written agreement of counsel.

XIV.
Request for Relief

WHEREFORE, PREMISES CONSIDERED, Plaintiff respectfully requests that the Court, upon trial by jury, enter a judgment against Defendants wherein Plaintiff recovers all of his actual and consequential damages, disgorgement of fees, exemplary damages, pre-judgment interest, post-judgment interest, attorneys' fees, interest, costs, and all other just relief.

Courtesy of Stephanie E. Kaiser, Partner, McGinnis, Lochridge & Kilgore LLP

ASPATORE